MOSS MOON

THE INSTITUTE OF AMERICAN INDIAN ARTS ANTHOLOGY SERIES

MASKED SPIRITS (1991)

VOICES OF THUNDER (1992)

IT'S NOT QUIET ANYMORE (1993)

BOTH SIDES (1994)

HOME IS IN THE BLOOD (1995)

VOICES AT DAWN (1996)

GATHERING OUR OWN (1996)

NOT THE LAST WORD (1997)

MOSS MOON

NEW WORK FROM
THE INSTITUTE OF AMERICAN INDIAN ARTS

1997-1998

EDITORS

JODY BARNES
CRYSTAL HENRY
TVLI JACOB
MARY SHAKESSPEARE
TIANAUSDI SHENANDOAH
DE ARMOND WILLIAMS

For information:

Creative Writing Program
Institute of American Indian Arts
P.O. Box 20007
Santa Fe, New Mexico 87504

This book, and others in the series, are available to the trade
through Small Press Distribution, 1341 7th Street, Berkeley,
California 94710; (510) 524-1668.

ISBN: 1-881396-14-2

POETRY

FICTION

NON-FICTION

DRAMA

POETRY

THE GRAVITATIONAL PULL OF A FISHBOWL

I have to clock in at the right time,
which is always
before the ship arrives
      with her cargo crates of goat horns
      shaped like long flat tears.

I descend in the near dark
before the sea haunts its fur lined belly
before we meet in the undertaker's blue city
      ornamented with silver fingernails etched like stars
      in a sky whose floor is fenced in with the humming
bladders of
      charred heifers licking
      away fresh   snow.

My frost pinched elbows
reach at the air like wings that do not fly.

I look into the lens of a fishbowl,
where my days spiral
      like a falling branch that pulls back its gravity.
      Reeling it in while thinking of the footprints leading
away into
      the thick green plaster of moss on stone.

Thinking:
      Spring,
      that moon with legs of silver water
      below
          black
ocean's hungry
      siphoned into the nose of soft veined sharks
      Death sharks who sign their names in braille
          on my moist back.

I hate the clock that snarls
      and whips its arms around me like a faded mattress.
         I bleed my left arm
            carving deep   gills.

BONE DUST

this season
starved my bones
into calcium chalk

tracing my outstretched arms
        reaching limbs
        which pinched cocaine from television snow

every hour smoked its swiveling tail
Frida Kahlo
stroked my palms

I panted
and asked God
        if he teethed as a child
        or if his fangs bled like mine

he rang
        the black telephone
        after the noon sun

        my arms: drying oars in a canyon stream

calendar crackling within my veins
        when I danced into blue television light
unsung
        looking over   Dinetah
 with milk film orbs
                through scotch taped trailer windows

paper bag skin
        chopped tongue
                bloodless fingers
                cannot be scraped away by paper thin metal

        the wind blows bone chalk
        over my body
                        drawn running

MOSS MOON

Her noose was carried
by shivering heat spines

spring lawn hoses
        nourish the moss
                inching along tall sunbeams
                from the pores of her swollen nose

        I saw this on channel 4

the news of her breath
snared tea bags from mud oceans
        fishes wept
        their saddle scales
                curled and flaked like deceased
                leaves

        white dry beaches
        crawled over slick faced cliffs
        last Autumn
                when we smoked her hair
                and peeled visions from
                blue turtle tails

ink pens stretched apart her thin legs
injected Penny Royal seeds
which leaved
        only on winter cemetery stones

my visions faded to blue blots
        shaped like Asian eyes
                the size of key-holes

She returned
small leafed maiden
green mane
        sandpaper waist

her noose quivered
sifting ash powder to wind
      above pale crows
        thrashing in gasoline puddles
        spiraling through cobalt rainbows

our long invisible rain coats
were not drought conscious
they missed the evening news
      when old retired clouds
      spat the ochre air of their peppered lungs

I danced in the black rain
clocks grew dizzy
black clouds fell away
      like sweat soaked olive sheets

and we refused our share of hibernating pills
      moss grew into a fuzzy green cancer dress
      wrapped tight around our necks

SKIN JACKET

I am fetus to the bed
        revolution sunday
        grease hissing mothers raise silver spatulas
        their screams cave into moans

        rain ascends
            moon dips
            her silver shawl into
                    black molten plastic
            dogs slip their tongues
            underneath squealing tires

 my nose dilates
        night smells like bubbling tar
        ink spills through open windows

I curl
        nibbling on jerky knees
        scrubbing christ from my loose ribs
        unwarmed on the kitchen table
        where shadows
            spit soaked my nipples
            while reaching for the light switch.

BLOOD CORSET

The star curtain did not return.

Fences rest firm against cactus hills
simmering like the veins of warm lampshades
        touching the night in my mouth
        coyote stirs his cave into foam
                and unearths my hand
        revealing the bones of my grandfathers.

I pull moans from my singed throat.
This pink wound that
licks the souring barbed wire until
coyote sits still on a cliff,
and scratches from his pores
        the buttons of my blood corset.

I cannot blink
        nor speak from my spitting wound
        the thickening eclipse
        paints my neck
                evening gray.

Blue crickets clutch their cut throats,
        their lung traffic crashes against the spooned palm of
        dusk.

A sun necklace blooms upon my shivering chest.
A spider's eyelid veils the smoky sky
and the stars refuse to open their black coats.

I dig into my pockets to find a stirring spoon
my cave sees the opening of a wall in the north ceiling
red bubbles stew within the siamese names
of our Mother and Father
                        their blood will not tar
                        nor gel

in my mouth where
my teeth teach my eyes
to touch the moving sound
      of Earth's dying scent.

BULLET

my brother's rifle
sank into desert dark

arroyos evicted shadows
when the bullet pierced

     and there was the soundless beast
     ears pulled back like clock arms
     crimson eyes pulsing
     pinched blind by a stem of light

his crescent eyes
resembled a crack in the floor
he howled
     and formed bull horns
     with rope thin arms
     against the pale platter faced moon

I knew then
he was designed for death
     his teeth were ivory triggers

the warrior in me slid
like warm candle wax
from my cold shivering feet

boot stomping song's
     white heartache
     our drumless ears
     felt like Waylon's chasm throat
        the wind blew through it all

black shirts could not hide
my sharp nipples or the incest within

     fuzzy moths glowered
     and scratched my tongue

     low beam headlights
        smothered the meandering night trail

SPEEDWAY

I envy the sun
     whose yellow sash
     jars my narrow orbs

undulating over the valley
     of diamond squares
     dotted blue, red, and yellow.

     The decorum of emergency.

I am more aware now,
while standing on hair thin stilts,
     the mined mesas hurling insults at caterpillars
     juniper air suffocating
          inside my caving lungs
     and the deep salmon sunset that burns
          hotter than the marred pistons in your father's
          muscle car.

I taste your salt
retreating in my blood like a moon
swallowed
and patched to the moving face of late night water.

My breath rides the pompadour of a New Mexican cloud,
     unthreading its sparrow lined jaw
     retrieving the dog that has chewed into its waist,
     and the eagles spiralling through its blooming blisters.

I am here,
above you like a preacher's unwilled erection
tracing your thigh with a burnt spoon.
thinking:

     how unfair it was of you
     to have kept me outside
          your needle.

THE STITCHED FLAT STONE

I cross the stitched flat stone
limping over tooth-sized pebbles
       gaining with each backward step
       the momentum of oncoming flu.

I pass the yellowing man
who deciphers my arm scars
these flesh ladders
       evidence of days
       wandering
           knee deep in the blue desert.

Asking,
       "Why do you strum my necklace grandfather?
           No one can unstitch the stitched spine
           or follow the sun who grazes the sky like a
           toothless shark."

He points his dry lips
to the shallow wet spine of the Rio Grande
saying that it is better to walk in the water
than to carry my tongue in the blowing wind.

He licks the whiskey neck:
       a fly fizzles
       he swallows
       and kicks the noose from the skeleton of my hands.

Touching my eyes
a white carousel circles a blooming black oval.

My hands unfold.
       My tongue slips into the wounded wet iris of a dry
       land.

HALO

1.

The sound of rain
drops
against the drooping bones of
      arthritic   hud-houses.

The weaving woman's child scrubs clear
      his knees
        splayed with the thin black paternal shadows
        of electric power lines.

Lines bowing like life-long servants
meshing their hair,
they uncover   our crushed feet.

2.

The child picks at his halo,
dissolving the dark into black pepper
eyeing
        the pull of the full moon
        on the water
        from whence our clans merged with flaked skin.

The halo's flourescence uncombs
the red mesas
and evens my palm with the coasting
      sky hawk and the rising blue.

The sun behind my thumb
keeps my blood from forming
      ice bergs in your hearts
      when Sumner's rank fingers are locked inside
      the stone used to pin the rooster's cry
        to the wind blown,
        wall of frozen sandstone eyes.

3.

My one child
> marks our twin names on the cells of fish.
> They are the stories of snow clouds shriveling like the
> palms
of our buried mothers
and the ruffling of our fathers
> against the barbed necks
> of lines drawn between pigment and pores.

We are only atoms trailing the carved skull wrapped inside a
> sunbeam.

> Dawn.

SO I SIT HERE

So I sit here
    Scotch for the time
        beer in-between
            attempt inebriation
                one can only try
    Drifting
    Drifting
        chance left behind
    So I sit here

    wonder wander where
        oblivion in toxifying
            my soul
            over
            and
            over

    You are always there
        and I sit here

    Drink Drank Drunk
butterflies will fly
        and socialize
            strange places
                strange people
        So I sit here
            empty
                Full glass
        have a seat
Bleed   With
        Me
        open your left eye
            straight or crooked
Cut   Deep
        Soul
jibber jabber bullshit

What the fuck
Close   Your
eyes
Cum to me with heart
open your right eye

cry cry
sigh
sigh

monotony..........monogamy
now
I sit here.

OAK AT DAWN

When I am old and crooked
like the oak at dawn
When my face is a black
silhouette, numb
in a hospital bed

When your baskets, pillows,
handmade quilts collapse into my lap
and the coyote no longer
hunts the buffalo in man made parks

Don't cry for me.

Thread your fingers together
in a peyote stitch and wipe red paint
on the forehead of transparent children
the way dogs lick their newborn

Double thread your family
Vicky and Jimmy on a peyote rattle
or eat your wife's womb to bare
no children

In the beginning
and end ghosts draw the lines
on my face, split in two
for my mix blood child
                    the man or the people?
                    the man or the people?
                        thousands and thousands

(Seeing the things through Grandpa's eyes)

                    I am old and crooked
                        an oak on the horizon at dawn

TAKE ME IN

this ring
belonged to you
on your slim brown finger
and rice paper skin
a ring
with one ball
of turquoise
that knocks at the door
after 1 am

carla
drunk
she wants to come in
she want to bring a ghost
with knives in both hands
"My grandma would let you in" she says
"But I never showed up at her door drunk" you say
and they roll away
to my parked car
and slash the tires instead

my old grandma
is left in her blindness
and braided orange necklace
300 miles from seeing Jesus
his over-worked back
        and sagging skin smells like a dirty washrag in the sink
        he is a thousand years old you said
        a corpse sitting on your shoulder
        or a violent cartoon character
dropping a 100 pound weight on your head
crushing you like the wi-ly coyote

her turquoise ring
that didn't fit his finger
melts between my thighs
or fingers
that leave bald spots on my head
jerk me back inside

shoot so-more
into my veins
until I taste onions
and lick the table
like a cat
the stray that appears
on your porch

                would you take me in
                feed me milk
                to strengthen my bones

                this ring
                the only thing left
                on my shelf
                my back bone

                                quiet rock of blue earth
                                that comes out
                                so you can go in

RESERVED TERRITORY

put some girls in it then
I want you to have some input
this is the core
i'm going to change it
maybe they're wearing church dresses
maybe this time they can be our mothers.
make it almost believable
thrown in the river, grandma's head
her bandanna and wrinkled core.

hold on, hey man you know
in church i just switch
the names around
flip the sexes and shoes
just be a good Indian
you know what I mean?

push it off, point the finger
at the center ring, some say
the Creator, Indian God
where have you been?
they've been burning our sage, John Wayne
sent smoke signals, the churches
are going to raise money.

it's not planned
to bring in the honor guards
the flags, the Great White Father
sits in the arbor and whistles
at the women's fancy dance
an abstract painting sets off
red watery lines run
black dots spread
blue tube squeezed and smeared.

I can see it
one step beyond the drunk guy
in the theater, *Indians were here first!*
just a fucked up Indian

like there's going to be anything
that hasn't already been said
in between crap edges it way
a companion flashing back
I don't know man.

                           the shriveled core can't help
                           pressure the language
                           pushing the ball of your eyes

I HAVE YELLOW SHE HAD WHITE

An irregular circle
yellow like the piss stain of a mattress
and daffodils in a long vase

yellow as the circle of fire reflecting
white paint walls and
rubber mouthed strangers in the afternoon

It's the yellow beaded triangle
on the baby's moccasin
smoked to a deep brown

The circle of fire lowers
into moths splashing
against bug lights

It's the yellow carton of film
tint of teeth
and hepatitis eyes

The white skinny stick
held between your fingers
like a blond hair lover beneath a devil moon

It's a yellowing treaty paper
and white kitchen walls of the old house
repossessed last year

Yellow, the color no child wishes to have
because it is a pee stain on the mattress
                        a wasp trapped behind a window

                                 the finality of words
                                 spoken by a stranger

LET'S PLAY A GAME: NAME THAT THING.

He plays around
with sound. Once he came
stayed and pointed:
   Poverty Point, Serpent Mounds, Group of
     Cut Copper Ornaments, Curiosities,
        Cannibals.

      He Said:
      Indian Art, Traditional
    Indian Art, Beadwork, Fry Bread,
    Black Hair, Short Nails, Curly
     Pubic Hair, Anus, Asshole,
      Suicide.

      He Called It:
      Dog, Petroglyphs, Lost
   And Loneliness, STD's, Genital Warts,
   Cankers, And Said
      I Had Cute Little Knees.

He's Beside Me
Naming You:
Geronimo, Tonto,
Pocahontas, Billy
Mills, Harry
Dick, Ute,
Paiute.

     He Even Speak A Language:
   Earth, Crust, Core, And Builds A House
     Where He Sleeps
    With His Wife In A King Size Bed.
   Rocks Laying Underground,
  Does He Know Sand And Gravel Too?

White Stripes,
Stretch Marks, Nipples,
Peach Fuzz,
Bacteria, Folds
Of A Penis Or Vagina And Poor
Blood Circulation.

Is This Why My Feet Are Cold?

Holding The Hand
Of My Tongue, My Thinking Cap,
My Life,

He Says *Yes Indian.*

That   Is   - Why
Your Feet   -   Are   -   Cold.

VANILLA CANDLE NIGHTS

I want to lazy the days away
close my eyes
dreaming of golden frog and sea horse hues

I want to hide the truth, close the hole
of a dolphin and watch his grey skin fade

I want to curl silk red ribbons
inside your chest
and listen to feet shuffle in the night

I want the umbilical cord around my neck
sea weed and checkered shells

I want to sleep again
in feathered beds
rolling spanish off my tongue

I want to recreate
in the stripes of a zebra

eat egg plant
and grow one foot taller

I want a big fat drunk
praying to the waning moon

I want to break the spine
of a book of eagles and wear it like a mustache

I want to shrink into a 1988 dime
shine silver
eat caviar and fold the skin of a baby

I want the fold of a skin of a baby

MELANIE CESSPOOCH_____

I want my mother's body
round lactating afternoons

I want a god damned miracle.

IS IT A MUSEUM

"they'll recognize you as Indian. if i could keep you in my left eye. the white light will never penetrate."

is it a museum
a burial ground
in which we live
     we toast.
          and sleep is when
          i wish
          i wouldn't wake.

it doesn't sound Indian
the way you use my words.
take out
The and And. place them
in the fold of my waist,
electricity for the world.
          wired up she says
          and the united nations
          still don't hear

but i still walk
20 to 25 minutes each day
another jewish holiday
for american minds
wrote my history and will try
to end it. with grandpa's leathers
already in the Indian museum.
          preservation on the reservation.
          who among us, will speak for
          the dead? your 3 year old
          or the sun?

and what do you know of the sun?
repeated text and Indian tales.
i heard it all the same the way
it appears in poems.

an Indian name. a mystic.
an 18th century medicine man.
well speak then
english
the official trade language

and my america
"teared" five thousand times
tears stream upside down
babies sliced in half. running
a live target for white soldiers.
                    my own people laugh

                    even that's not appropriate.
                    fat sagging from bones.
                    Indian bones.

and you dare ask me
if i'm qualified. i shouldn't want
children. talk to the mayans
if you can find them in text
or institutions, and repeat
                    save the earth 20 10
                    (we will never)
                    save the earth two thousand ten
                    the american campaign for presidents.

the government referees tribal boundaries
and now the navajo and hopi
grow ears of corn and evil eyes.
both nations cheer.
NFL football out of season.
                    the Indians refuse to huddle

but continue to break
and break cradles
not yet ready to birth.

grandma rocks, and for years
she rocked. she's not crazy,
she knows a twinkle
is the reflection of white light.
she thinks to sing a death song.

slow
the drum the drum
is beating too fast

THE FOX THEATRE

sitting on a hard gray carpet, the fox theater
                              buzz buzzz
horn singing a jazz song in the back
                            da da da da da da dah dah
                            boom boom boom
a drum unlike the heart beat drum of a powwow
maybe that's why I am so alone
like a potted flower or a glassed in snake at the zoo
                        ready to strike
                      my lightning
                          strike down
                              the building
                              florescent light
                              black
                    buzz buzz buzzz buzzz
                    of the audience standing hunched
screech screech and piano keys, is this sophistication? hair
      salon top. an alias for the people inside.
come over. come in. we're open 24 hours a day. convenient. the
      new Instead product for women. selling me. pulling that
      horn in my throat, weakening my voice so as not to talk
                      anymore.
I'm just woman
what a boring title
your voice won't last like a rainbow after rain
you want to be beautiful
Madonna, Virgin Mary
                    a marble statue taking up space and
                          energy of ants
                    looking for sugar and dirt to plant a
                    home.
                            breaking their tailbone
                            to get out of the buzzing
                            and heat of day

I want to break of my glass case
                    my Reebok shoes and walk home
                    barefoot
                        6 hours from here, the fox

theater, Boulder, Colorado.
my glass- a rainbow trout in the Boulder
Library

          like   non chalant
    swimming   society
                  flip flip

who is it?
       flip flip
here wait. let me take a picture. click
here wait. it's an interesting color
                 Black.
to hide, or STAND OUT, attract all persona
    sun, moon, gravity, electrons
                 buzz buzzz
where does it come from? point! it doesn't matter. not here in
    black.

        we have no teeth, no tongue, no people
you want to make up 3 and 4 letter words, name your
    neighbors cat
and follow
the curve of its back
the hair shedding
in your hand

        I'm just a woman.
what a boring title
look in the bathroom mirror, silver
        spit aqua in the sink
I'm going to sit quiet
below your black stage
    inside your gut
    behind your liver
    the time you raped your daughter
    or slammed the family car off the road
        eeeeerrrrttt!

MELANIE CESSPOOCH_____

I'm going to sit in black pants
sponge your words running like rain in the gutter
your finger skills, de-bone chicken, clothing your imagination
your porno's and TV.
                   clapping clap clap
                   the way I clap a mosquito in midair

I'm going to clip your male lions
your white eyes and giant teeth
                   slurping
I leave you
flat and broken
a mattress and sore shoulders, dirty hair
here have some hairspray
let's start up again. open the set.
open up and say "AH"
scissors, okay. -clip
              that hanging section
             in the mouth
             looking nasty wiggling its hips
                       clip-
                             Thank You.

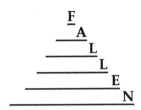

INSTIGATING A REBELLION
THEY FELL UNDER HIS WINGS
HE WAS THE MOST BEAUTIFUL
HE WAS THE MOST CORRUPTIBLE
CREATOR HE ONCE WAS
DESTROYER HE NOW IS

HIS FATHER LOVED HIM
HIS FATHER EXPELLED HIM
THROWING HIM INTO THE FIERY PIT
PAIN WAS HIS LUST
HATRED WAS HIS WEAPON
PRIDE WAS HIS ARMOR

MORNING STAR SHINED BRIGHTEST IN HEAVEN
FELT EVEN BRIGHTER IN THE FLAMES
HE'S SO GODDAMNED GORGEOUS
HARD TO RESIST
ELOQUENT SPEAKER
AN ARMY WOULD FOLLOW HIM ANYWHERE

A BALANCE
"IT'S A ROLE I HAVE TO PLAY
HIS WILL
MY HONOR
WOULD FATHER
ACCEPT THE RETURN OF THE PRODIGAL?"

MURDERERS
CONVICTS
THEY ALL NEED A PLACE TO STAY
HE TOUCHES THEM ALL
CARESSES THEM
WITH HIS MOIST HAND

"SOMETIMES
I'D LIKE TO RETURN
WOULD I BE WELCOMED?"
HE SMILED A WIDE CURVED SMILE
EMBODYING PERFECTION
DANTE'S RIGHT:

"BETTER TO RULE IN HELL THAN TO SERVE IN HEAVEN"

NECROPHELIA

his eyes stared upward
–nothing
she caressed his hard cold flesh
'the perfect body,' she thought

motionless he remained
she tasted his skin
her tongue licked his nipples

as he stiffened
Copulation began
not once did he look at her
She pressed on

Her sweat dripped onto him
rolling down like a tear

"My heart can beat for both of us,"
she told him
"I love you–
Love you forever.
You don't have to say anything.
I can feel it as your life enters me."

An orgasmic charge rushed through her spine

His eyes closed.

SHE IS A DAUGHTER

she is a daughter
she is a mother
she is a sister
she is grandmother

her young ample body
walking in the snow
feet bleeding
face going numb

ghosts on horses
telling her to move along
she stumbles
she takes her mother's hand
she will not survive the walk
walking towards the sunset
Death will find her tomorrow
embraceable Death

her son argues with her more often
he goes out drinking
not coming home for days
last night he stole her car
never returning
pain and tears
across a highway of shattered glass

her brother the young warrior
will not come home today
the burial ceremony has begun
it is said that he fought for america
fighting for a country
that destroyed his ancestors
she weeps as they raise his body
fearless he was
she misses him

alone on a porch
no one visits her anymore
in her eyes you glimpse what she has seen
her face tells the story of her life
each line
each wrinkle

the knowledge that she carries
the visions she has seen
unshared
unknown
a life faded away
a history gone
she weeps no more.

THE COWBOYS WIN AGAIN

John Wayne, Buck Rogers, Superman, and The Lone Ranger
These were my childhood heroes
Who else would there be?

Sure, Tonto was an okay guy
but The Lone Ranger had all the neat things
He wore a black mask
He carried two guns
He had the better horse

Who else did I have to look up to?
Burt Lancaster? Chuck Conners?
shit, these guys didn't even have good makeup

When the Cowboys fought the Indians
we were supposed to root for the cowboys
the Indians were ruthless savages

This Sunday I'll root for the Cowboys
when they play against the Redskins

The Cowboys are America's team

"I don't feel wrong in taking this great country away from them.
Our so-called stealing of this country was just a matter of
survival. There were a great number of people who needed new
land, and the Indians were selfishly trying to keep it for
themselves."

When I thought about tough
I thought about John Wayne
I wanted to be like John Wayne
strong and noble
never taking shit off nobody

I admired all the great people in history
I remember George Washington
Who could not tell a lie
He once threw a coin across a river

Then there was Abraham Lincoln
He was always honest
He brought together a divided nation

The Indians and the pilgrims shared a dinner together
It is now called Thanksgiving

Pocahontas seized fighting with the Virginians
then she married a white man and moved to Europe

Walt Disney made a movie about her
she saved John Smith's life
and fell in love

I don't remember reading about that in the history books

Russell Means played her father
wasn't he a part of the American Indian Movement at one time

Then there was Andrew Jackson
He must have done some great things
He's on the twenty dollar bill

Ted Turner, Jane Fonda, Lou "Diamond" Philips, Robert Redford

They represent our people?

Sitting in a HUD home
looking for the next beer buzz

Superbowl party tonight
plenty of drugs, plenty of booze

The Cowboys win again

MY SISTER

my sister wants to be blonde
she wears a bleached wig
that was found at a thrift store
she sings Madonna songs
wearing T-shirts
that shows her flabby stomach
revealing her belly button
once, she wore makeup
to make her skin lighter
mother got mad
she's too young to paint her face like that

my sister wants to be a Mexican
she wears red bandannas
across her eyebrows
and oversized tan Dickie's
she says she's going to date Miguel
because he drives a low rider
with hydraulics
causing the car to go
two feet off the ground

my sister wants to be a Nubian princess
ebony skin
and bright red, yellow, green colored clothing
she doesn't wash her hair
she says
that's how she gets her dreads
she dates a black man
named Michael
his penis isn't as big
as she thought it would be

my sister wants to be everything

everything but an Indian

UNTITLED #1

What is done
-undone
cut back
to black
gestated eyes
prepare to see

CLEAR?

whores
dance around
 the swollen
jet black---

flies circle
picking the coat
collecting reds and blues
stench runs deep

breath
circles the nostrils

grey dried
lips pulsate
            blue
turning cold
in each passing moment

blocked vision
through crooked
ashened
twigs
the marble
            world
crumbles to
            stained
            black
curtains

who is your mother?
abusing the child
          severely
black lungs
          disfigured
bones
    turning to sawdust.

SHE WALKS ALONG CHERRY COVERED STREETS

She walks along Cherry covered streets
cobalt moonlight shines her way
Her mainstay of ecstacy
never dampens her fear
her body heat
causes a glistening
after the short minutes
of an unmasked cold touch
escaped into her

Her dreams are of sapphire's blooming
and fire without heat
She holds her dreams
between cardboard plates
unopened to multiple eyes

secrets known
are quite deadly

She's a pinwheel
spinning along the floor
rain drops and tears
splash the lace white walls
Blue smoke escapes her nostrils
She wants to collapse
unstoppable she leaps
unstoppable she flies
letting go
letting go

Her icy blue eyes
can penetrate through you
quicker than a silver bullet
Crimson lips
burn your tongue
inhaling your life
taking your breath
stilling your heart

Beware of her dreams
beyond her control
powerful words
unstoppable
bleeding black
upon thin leaves

to decipher her dreams
can spin a vortex
into darkness

a small silver spark
can conjure up a bright yellow sun
through a dark gray cloud

curved colored lines
she reaches for
hoping to touch them
hoping to bathe in them
"Is it true
what they say
about those ghostly images?"

her heart beats like a distant drum
her ears explode
thunder claps
and silver lightning
to disperse

smell the magnum
taste the silence in the air

SHOULD'VE TAKEN THE OFF RAMP

thirty minutes out of my way
the cracked highway smothers into darkness
smells like damp oil or burning tar
the rust colored Ford stutters
coughing

"You're innocent when you dream"

Tom Waits
does a somersault
for the fourth time

"Fuck," i tell myself
dead town
empty well-lit stores
rush by me
i don't slow down
cracked dashboard
shimmers green light
illuminates a beautiful smile

if i weren't driving
i'd be caught in a stare

instead i take the photograph
roll down the window
she becomes a flower
soars from my hand

becomes a dream
in the middle of the day
scattered tangent remembrences
unclear
crystal glitter

on the window
the wheel
can take
a circular motion

should've taken the off ramp

THE LAUGHING MOTHER

Her tongue is paper
and a cricket kicks
in the palm of her hand

I sit and stare at the women
with the archaic smile

Her eyes tumbleweeds in an ocean
She spits blood on Sunday mornings
and words coil around her arched fingers

She is tribal
She is a killer
She is unkind

She is perplexed with iron statues
and ivory towers
spitting metal on mahogany

I sit and stare at the women
with the archaic smile

She is laughing at me
I am her uprising

A negation
my reflection.

OASIS

There is an Oasis
of knowledge
within
the
springs of understanding.

Beneath the dunes
of the
desert sands
there is
a
lake of wisdom
that will
make you bloom
into a
beautiful
desert flower,
in
the
heat of the
day fire
sun.

Deep within
this Oasis,
there
are
gentle chocolate
kisses
that need to burn
within
the empty
souls of
humanity.

To drink
from
this Oasis
one must
kneel down
to
unexpected light
winter snows

One
must
then
lick up
the
melted
chocolate kisses
into the
void
of one's
human soul.

REMEMBER

Once there was a man, like a bird, free from birth. One day someone came and caught him. Like a bird he was put into a cage. Generations after generations, the bird was told many bad things about him by his owner. Generations after generations, the bird was told many good things. The bird was even given a new name by his owner

After a long time hearing bad things about him by his owner, then hearing many good things about him by his owner, he began to feel happy about all the good things said about him. He had even forgotten the condition of his environment that surrounded him and the freedom of his birth. He even started to answer to the new name given him.

One day, the door of the cage was left open, the bird with shallow eyes looked upon the opening and was puzzled. He was caged so long, that the open door of freedom seemed like captivity and the closed door of captivity seemed like freedom. The next day the door was closed and the bird came to realize he had died.

CLAY

Cool and porcelain
no rattling
no warm lips pressed to delicate sides
blank and sterile
a hospital toilet

waiting alone
at an unlit *firmata*
for an orange bus
full of voices that
turn words
into baked potato
burning a foreigner's
mouth

allowing
bourbon flavored
tongues to shove
into tired swirls of
inner ear

where the collar bone
meets the neck
a notch
of longing that is
too lazy
to do anything
but grace the covers
of fashion magazines

Friday nights
spent
driving a powder-blue
Oldsmobile
watching from interstates'
brightly lit windows
smiling faces trapped
inside a sour kindergartner

crying to a mirror
a test tube bubbling over
acid then base, base than acid
like reading
War and Peace
at age eleven

a locker room
after twelve hours of riding a stationary
bicycle
and arriving nowhere

Ugly, Blatant, and Needy
a quarter
bobbing
in the *Shoawnoa* river

HEAT FALLS FROM LIMBS

The purple evening is my shade
only dust makes my face brown
sun at rest in the horizon's bed
     you did see me when I hid

Fire is the heart of smoke
smoke the whispered flame
flame the fruit of lusting
     lusting the soil of ash

Blue morning wakes my dawn
dawn is dusk with yellow face
moon waits beyond westward hills
     you have seen my flesh wrinkle

Rain on the mothers to be
wombs the force in life
life the lips speak madness
     Madness a cold twisted shame

Day, night, and the black cool eye
     haze fights for clear winter's barb

Bastards badly born
     hands and hives do wax

Gold and Silver are not wise
     spruce and hickory not prized

Bark the dogs at me and mine
     kick there carcasses from the mind

Blue sweet grass wakes
alone in the corn fields
a stiff dog, a pillow
     smell of cows in the air

Great winds tear with silk talons
     Heart drops to bowels

4AM

A cold breath consumes the flames
freezing raincoats the earth's dark gray fur
the seasons believe in the reaper now
because he whispers in their hair

The black night they do not ponder
crackling in the mist
firing out words of warning
deaf, dumb, and blind
      The day is dawning

INSURED BY SMITH & WESSON

Lungs tremble with every puff of air
Knees, legs, thighs rattled in the bones
A fly buzzes close to distract me
Years flash repeatedly

Stale Coors fragrant the air as he snoozes
    like a baby
Strands of brown hair pasted with sweat
Crickets hum his gnarled nerves straight
Their chirps higher with tension

Staring over tender lumps
Blood rushes to repair eggplant cheek bones
Shrugging tears, runny nose on a
    tattered stained shirt
"Fuck you!" through ballooned lips

It fits like tight Levis, the clip
    echoes with a click
A deep breath, shoulder aches as she
    cocks with ease
An instant races from the trigger to the
    elbow and stabs

A RAY OF THE SUN

A ray of the sun peaks over the mountain
A cold trickle of water slides down to the
    nearby stream
furry animals come out of their hiding places

Gusts of smoke as you exhale the evening air
Billowing dust clouds emerge after the car passes
In the midst of it all, you see figures everywhere

Open fireplaces, laughing children, wrinkled faces
Salty drymeat stew and salty tears of
    warm embraces
Odors of Hills Brothers and frybread

Dust of iron ponies on a hot night, drown the drumbeat
Blanketed figures in the moon lit paths
    scurry to the lodge
Traffic slows as the songs increase

Whistles blow in unison, and the dance proceeds
A face lightens as if turning the knob of a Coleman lamp
Sage, cedar and dust fill the air

Fireplaces burn out, one by one
Spirals of smoke entwine to the stars
White powder hisses as the water interrupts
    the calm of the night

A little rest before the Sunrise
Open mouths, tongues wave and let out a holler
Murmurs in the tipi, Shhhhhh

ONE FINE DAY

Spotlights shine through the mountains
Fresh tracks race in the dried dust
Meadowlarks sing their songs

Newborn horses kick at each other
A tipi opens to the sun
Stretching , yawning as they talk

    A sadness, creeps by in a
    spinning whirl of dust
    Aching to be among them

    Cedar rises slowly as you pull it over you
    murmurs chant in rhythm
      as the spiral slowly dances upward

More, laughter as the little ones awake
puppies bark, biting at tails
The sun stands in the middle

Waves of dust intrude only but a second
sagebrush fragrant the land
while peppermint hides by the river

LOVE HURTS

Cold wooden floor sticky with beer
Blurrred view distracted by a hairline headache
Cradling my head like a baby
Blood dries tightly on my face

How long did I lay there?

Ribs crunch with every breath
Wooden oak chairs watch me, but can't help
Black reflects a distorted thing

     Its face shadows of purple
     Bulging eye sockets, zig zag nose
     Almost up, it falls, skin screams

Leaning over the sink, blue soft
     cloth kisses the hurt
Ivory overcomes blood/beer mixtures
Diamonds shine from the scalp
Maroon lava as the slivers are pulled

"You know I love" smoke rings twist to swirls

THOUGHTS OF BILLOWING WIRE

I sit
in my duct tape
kimono
he coaxes linoleum
off the floor.

If I had
a weathered nail
I'd jab it
into his foot
until blood flowed
from his ears.

The incompleteness
of a staple gun
reminds me
of bronze light fixtures.

The smell of
the cedar tool box
sends memories of
broken glass
thrashing.

If there were
a pillar
of concrete between us
I'd slam it down
on him.

LOOSING GOYA DA YENS DIH

Sometimes I hear do'dis
calling her name;
the syllables tangling in my
hair like burdocks.
Her tears stick to my face
like the maple sap I once sipped.
Strawberry stained fingers
stretching to grasp my clenched fists.

sometimes she dances on my face,
her pussy willow toes tickling my chin.
Shoving dogwood blossoms
up my nose to wake me,
her foreign screams crash
to the floor.

One time she gave me
a nightmare to keep.
Kivas, sweat lodges, and longhouses
breaking my bones; my grandma
in each door
yelling the strange language.
Breath sucked out of me,
nameless, in her forests.

She whispers my name;
ashes from the sacred fire
scattering.
I reach for it , for her.
Knowing she is
my survival.

LEAVE ME ALONE

We're deviant relations
our blood is of
convenience to you

tell me then why
your grandma
was my great

only one of yours died
warm blood melted
masses of snow
I don't feel saved

you smother my damnation
with words of love
your mind set
sickens me

I don't need your sad history
of death
I've got Wounded Knee
(it's really yours too)

the light of
your heaven
pierces my eyes
you think I'm
ignorant

I'm not a sheep
my beliefs
are strong

I leave you
to your plagues
leave me
to my prophecies

Leave me alone.

YUCCA ROOT

Tell a story from the beginning is what elders say;
there she stands on the deserted ruins.

Wipe the tears, erase the fears;
watch my breath evaporate in the winter frost air.

Walk with me, your moccasined feet, my Nikes.
Children chase each other, specks of dust in my eyes.

Wipe your nose, touch your toes.
Ye man of little faith.

Then it all happened one rainy day.
That woman knocked on my HUD house door.

INDIAN

I am not an Indian. I am not Navajo.
I am Dineh!

>Yellow sweat
>from my body, cascades like the sworls
>>in my finger tips, down the thigh
>>of an unvirtuous river.

>My footprints,
> narrow arcs, paste themselves in the bosom,
>of a red sandstone desert.
>>Sacred, beauty colors the blue and white
>>spinning rainbows, with
>splintered green yucca.

My feet,
trace the chicken claw of a blue lizard,
saluting the sun.

>Saluting in a white star bathed, desert.

>I inhale dust off pollinated cactus–a fire of purple
under a pale canopy;
My tongue scrapes the teeth
of a desert pear, enjoying seedy
flavor.

I peel away the tint of a Carson night. I peel away
crawling infection, and stay cold.

>Reduced, none.
> Dineh maps I follow, yellow flowered cactus
I eat.
>Black streaks caught in the wind
lick my forehead, weaving Ni-szhoni (Beautiful)
sand, into my eyes.

I do not want *to* be an Indian.
I am not an Indian.
I am song. I am tears. I am father, mother.
I am black lightning on blue diamond.
I am an insect, without a flock.
I am barbs stretched across winged expanse.   I am Dineh.

PARTED

is memorizing a happy
song, too joyous to
remember

or

drinking the sky without
the smell of earthy rain-clouds,
to kiss a petal for a

lamenting beauty in black,
whose ebony eyes of crow
FALL under an indifferent sky

flashing,

days beyond joy
when politeness opened doors,
into sunsets of green reflections,

clinging

to the sewn underbelly
of sheepish clouds,
brackish in their evenflow.

Dreaming

where kneeling willows caress
aching stone, dissolving alongside
withering pearls on a receding bank,

which

is just a dissipated path,
filled with exposed
brilliance, hungry to be
set in gold

SOMETIMES

Sometimes, a jeweled star is

        hidden behind the rippled peaks,

                of a shaded mountain silhouette.

Where the violet fingers twist

        a thread of frosted blanket

           out of an earthen bed.

Sometimes, the tide is without a reflected

        moon, pulling the sandy bottom,

           into a lovers cloudless arms,

Dreaming of Galapagos shell, upon

        an empty shore, drawn by

           salted air into an un-molesting sea.

Sometimes the world stops revolving

        even though melancholic wheels

           persist in their revolutions.

CRIMINAL

       I am alone with the cobwebs, looking down at the varnished floor which executes lightning, as if raked leaves have been punished.
Eyes sitting around the navel of a swelled courtroom dissect my cerebreum.
I am in a forest of crucifixion, lined with stitched crosses, clothed in elastic robes; a robe I soon shall fashion.

       _I_ am judged by _your_ sitting God, who bows to the scales of _demos_ , that interpret my resistance, as rusty hinges on a coffin, made for an unborn child. And the seat of **your** God spins, by propelled, shiny green plastic mechanics, which operate under a scarf, woven from the ideas of gold capped mountains.

       I am it; the one parted from the rocks and grasses, which shift their eyes, and prick their drooping ears with the Manifesto, my communal entity.

       And now I am I; facing the snarling sheep who click their soiled toes in time, at the engagement of steel on stone.

TASTING THE HEROIN

tasting the heroin in my nostrils as it tickled plumed feathers on
my platelets was like touching Buddha with Mr. Clean tattooed
on my meatless ass
handing back white chance meant there would be zero to come
it tasted brown like warm molasses
without the blood of maples to flavor steely appetite
pecking the drip pans for more warm molasses I lost my feather

it flickers the quivering eyelids with narcoleptic lullabies tuned to
the tune of
Cheshire poppies
wavering on
the soles on lethargic Peruvians

it tasted like smoke in my ears as
hollering waters slither with the undercurrents of
brief numb death in mortality   brief sick death in mortality
brief sleep in mortality
g o n e

SUN

You Star, descend a view, like a fire fly, landing
under purple flower, illuminating a star within a star.

You Star shelter falling leaves, from frosting limbs, detaching
gliding towards a golden circle, spinning loosely
holding the leaf in a red–orange balance.

You Star. I grasp you in the iris of a faded orb. Blinded
by a beauty held only in the fingers of a slipping memory.

You Star, I am enclosed in the palm of
your charted column, supporting the earth
in a wrinkled chasm.

Darkness, darkness, encases my withering
body. For the blink of an eye I would touch.

There is no more constellation which I can
connect a glimmer of happiness, it has fallen
into welcoming emptiness, which slowly disperses.

You are not purple flower. You are not my
nightmare, which follows my reality out of my unconsciousness.

You are lost smile. Lost to an eternity of frown
embodying untruthful whispers, which create my
descent towards untilled soils.

You Star, are, our map, lined with
roads which lead to mirror facing mirror.

LONELY BUT NEVER DEPRIVED

Once I had, honey morning sunshine.
She is an echo of shadow, a
distant embraced thought.

Judas kiss would've admired her amber
                                    embrace.
I am accepting to this truth, as Fallen One accepted
Cosmopolitan jealousy.

She is gone, now, crows under my
eyes shake salt off their wings

I walked through a peach scented
garden for her,
plucking fire colored ripeness, with
a green flavor, and was reminded
of loss. I licked a fuzzy peel,
dismayed of its lack, virtue.

The stars are a love poem, which read
like Razumikhin, in Chapter eleven.
A poem written with nicotine fingers, imbuing gold
words, that do not shine, shaking the turning color
from my leaves.

Bitter, bitter, bitter, is my tongue
from the lemons I found in a perfect
bosom of deception. I have melted into
the oils of the Great Masturbater, and
am spent like a muse without
mystery.

You are distress, clothed in a violet halo of angelic origin,
you were my velvet, clinging to the rose. And now I
deny myself the pleasure of memory, thinking you are still mine.
Still mine, still mine, still mine, like this melodramatic rant of
expression.

DOLPHIN

i drink the ocean of your body
and taste the salt of your curvature
along with the forgotton sailors
of which your sea does not remember
the waves under your skin tremble
at my footsteps outside the door
is this still so
you engulf the space between my ears
as i drown at the bottom of your precious spine
i swim in your brown eyes
when you smile and turn around
i ache at the thought of not growing old
within your shores
where swollen kelp reaches outside
the floating blue
trying to grasp the roof of the world
shining light peeps through the ebony
of your hair
and hooks my eye
the darkness streaks across my face
and settles into a rainbow
deep purple blue and green
maps the crevices
of my widening lips

COLD

In a white morning of frost,
I taste the colors of summer's cool moisture;
at the moment the sun's fingers dissolve into a purple-blackness.
The lazy snowflakes dance before they are absorbed.
I drink from a cold memory, and shiver with the
millions upon millions of crystals, enveloping
a pine stump outside my wordless window.
I envy the snow, falling out there, laughing to each other.
Waiting below, melting sisters silently giggle
goddbye, goodbye, goodbye.
In a flaking world of snow and words I cannot choose
the words I long to describe the falling of me.
I feel the stars calling to the snow outside. They say,
"Remain in our fading light, kiss our empty breath."
Dropping eyes remain outside,
as the descending plasma
inside my listless brain freezes.

EMERGE

Manuelito, did you sing a song?
Was it a beautiful song, like purple sunflowers, blooming
in a yellow dew? Did you mouth the lyrics,
as the People were led to disaster, like dibe'(sheep)
to the fire?

Was it like the emergence? Like the insects
gathering, ascending in haste,
when the turkey's tail fanned
the swell of immoral, waters.

Or...

A beetle, rising from magenta depths.
Swallowing the blue air.
Beetle, without legs
                    without wings,
                              without sight.
Scattered, on volcanic, green cliff.
Scattered on salted ice.
Scattered like the voices,
which death turned to ear,
and hate turned to acceptance.

Barboncito.
Warrior, where did the dust in
your hair fall, when you shook
your head in defiance, of
a blue coated law?

The People fell, as infants.
They fell, trying to stop the slaps, like
children before they fall.

The women, kept their eyes down.
They kept their eyes down!
They kept their eyes on the memories
of scalpless children.

FICTION

PAPA

My Papa lifted the binoculars to his eyes, slowly scanning the treetops. We'd been standing on the shore of this lake for fifteen minutes. My curiosity had long since given way to what my mother called "the fidgets."

"Papa, do ya see 'em?" I asked, tugging at his pant leg.

Papa ignored me. Sighing, I wandered over to a big rock and settled myself onto it. The rock was warm, its surface smooth. I picked a strand of Canary Grass and tried to make a whistle, the way I'd seen my uncles do, holding the blade between the outside edges of my thumbs and blowing hard into the little opening made by my bent knuckles. The sound that resulted was that of a deathly ill duck with an intestinal disorder. Figuring practice makes perfect, I attempted to play "She Loves You", pausing to sing the yeah-yeah-yeah parts out loud. Taking a deep breath I was about to launch into an encore of "Hurdy Gurdy Man" when, glancing up, I caught Papa's eyes looking at me, his brows knit together in a slight frown. Embarrassed, I ducked my head and let the piece of grass fall from between my hands.

My Papa was an awe-inspiring man, especially in his tan DNR uniform, stern enough that one small look could quiet a restless ten-year-old. I watched his broad back as he searched for the Bald Eagle that was nesting on the other side of the lake. Papa was a Game Warden and every couple of days he'd check to make sure no one had hurt the eagle or its eggs - something he called "poaching" - a word that caused me much confusion, since my favorite thing to eat for breakfast was poached eggs and toast. Worried that my mother was breaking the law by being one of those "damn poachers," I asked Papa about it one day. He assured me everything was on the up and up, that was a different kind of poaching. As he walked away I swear I heard him laughing.

Suddenly, a shrill cry came from above and behind us, startling me so badly I nearly fell off the rock. I craned my neck in time to see the eagle glide into view and swing out over the lake. I watched in awe as it soared smoothly, its wings opened to full span.

"Papa," I asked quietly, "what do eagles eat?"

Without turning around he answered in his low,

grumbly voice, "Fish." Then, shrugging he added, " little girls."

Glancing above me I moved closer and hooked my fingers though one of his belt loops. Papa lowered the binoculars and turned away from the lake.

"We gotta go up to The Dells. There's a troop of Boy Scouts comin' down the river. I'm suppose to meet 'em, give 'em a little talk." He jerked his head toward the truck. "Let's go and see some real live white people."

The sandy path that led away from the lake was only wide enough for one person at a time, so I followed behind my grandfather. His boots left deep, waffle-like prints in the sand and I hopped from one print to the next, all the way back to the truck. Papa drove a big, dusty pick-up truck with a red bubble light on the dashboard and a police radio with a lot of little knobs that sat on the hump of the drive shaft. He also had a gun in a leather holster that was kept in the locked glove compartment. I could count the times I actually saw him wearing the holstered gun on one hand. When Papa strapped on his gun, you knew there was badness happening somewhere on the Rez.

Being a Game Warden was dangerous business. I remember hearing about a Game Warden in a neighboring county who, one night, caught a young guy shooting deer from the road. The young guy was crazy or maybe he was drunk. When the Warden tried to take his gun away, the young guy shot him and killed him. Then he dragged the body into the woods and buried it in a shallow grave. I remember overhearing my mother and uncles talking about the crazy guy and how, before he buried the body, he cut the Game Warden's head off and left it in his car. It took the police exactly seven days to find the murderer. My Papa wore his gun everyday that week.

I opened the door of the truck and climbed up onto the dusty tan seat. The cab of the pick-up smelled of English Leather and tobacco and Brylcreem. I hummed along to the 8-track of Charlie Rich as we jounced along the twin wheelruts that served as a road.

"When we get to the Dells can I go swimmin'?" I asked

hopefully.

The Dells is a spot where the cold, clear water of the Wolf River tumbles through a granite gorge and shifts down two sets of rapids. I was a strong swimmer and unafraid of the water, I loved to paddle out into the swift current under the falls. Sometimes I'd swim upriver, the force of the water holding me back until my arms ached with effort. Then I'd flip over onto my back, letting the rushing water whisk me downstream. Papa always told me to go feet first down the river and to keep my toes up, level with my shoulders. I wasn't quite sure why he thought I should do this, but Papa had a way of telling you to do things so that you just did it without asking any questions.

"No, the water is really high right now and the current is too strong. I don't want you playing in the water." Papa said, not looking at me. He was too busy driving. When he drove he'd push his cowboy hat way back on his head, then he'd lean way over the steering wheel with his arms crossed. Kinda like he was leaning on a fence somewhere instead of driving a pick-up.
Papa was a bad driver, probably because he steered with his armpits and never watched the road. He was always looking up at the treetops or off into the woods.

I sighed and frowned, hoping maybe the Wescott kids would be at The Dells, so I'd at least have someone to hang around with. The Wescott's had a little foodstand that sold sodas and hamburgers to the rafters that came downstream or tourist that would come to take pictures of the Dells. Papa pulled through the sandy square where the people who came to look at the river and walk in the woods parked their cars.

Since my papa was Game Warden he didn't have to park by all the other cars. He pulled right up and parked next to the little food stand. Papa stepped out of the Pick-up, hitched up his pants, righted his cowboy hat and took in his surroundings. I stood near the tailgate, waiting for him to tell me if it was ok to go play, but he just walked past without saying anything. He stepped up onto the little wooden porch of the food stand and leaned an elbow on the counter. His face was dark brown, with high cheek bones and lines around his eyes that would crinkle up when he laughed. He looked like some one from 'Gun Smoke'-Marshall Matt Dillon, maybe-with his stitched pointy boots and his hat and his hand-tooled leather belt with the big silver buckle.

Papa nodded to Mr. Wescott, who was sitting on a stool, swatting flies with a much used fly swatter.

Mr. Wescott nodded back. "Hap."

Everyone always called my papa Happy, or just Hap, I don't know why, he never seemed particularly happy. Most of the time he was down right crabby.

"Lot a rafters?" Papa asked.

"Nah," Mr. Wescott grumbled. "The water's too damn high and too damn fast."

"There's a troop of Boy Scouts comin' down today." Papa glanced at his watch. "Should be here pretty soon."

"Christ, people are crazy. I wouldn't let MY kids on that river. It's too damn high." Mr. Wescott swatted a fly for emphasis.

"That's what I tried to tell 'em, but the Troop Leader wouldn't listen to me. I figured I'd meet 'em here. If any of 'em didn't wanna go on, they could get out and I could take 'em back to their bus."

I sat down on one of the stools that was actually just a big log stood on end, and started to pick at the scab on my knee. I asked if I could please have a soda. Mr. Wescott didn't even wait for my grandpa to answer. He slid open the big red metal Coke cooler next to him and fished me out a can of grape Jolly Good. My favorite. I looked up at him to say 'thanks' but he was looking past me, over my head.

"Ho, here come your boys, Hap." Mr. Wescott jutted his chin toward the river. Coming around a bend were three blow up rafts. There were four boys and one adult in each boat. Everyone was paddling like crazy, fighting the swirling current to get to shore. As they neared our side of the river bank, they disappeared behind a huge upshoot of stone. Papa straightened up and stepped off the porch. Glancing back at me he said, "wait here."

I nodded. I had my Jolly Good. I wasn't going anywhere. Besides, Mr. Wescott was usually good for a pack of Juicy Fruit, especially if I'd help him build a fire so the Boy Scouts could warm up a little. I watched Papa move away from me, and disappear behind the out cropping of rock.

I hopped off the stump and started picking up sticks and dry leaves. I put them in the dug out firepit. Mr. Wescott came out of the stand, searching his pockets for his lighter. He had a silver Zippo, just like my grandfather. In no time at all the sticks and leaves were crackling loudly. He started to stack the bigger pieces of wood over the burning kindling in a Teepee shape. Meanwhile, one by one, the scouts were straggling up from where they pulled ashore, following one of the adults. They didn't look like they were have too much fun. They looked cold and wet. When they saw the fire they hurried over, jostling each other for a good spot near the brightly burning flames.

Reclaiming my seat, I looked over the pitiful bunch of shivering boys. I envied them their uniforms, their brightly stitched Merit Badges and their cool yellow scarves. I wished I could join the Boy Scouts. I'd have that fire building badge cinched, not to mention the swimming and the Indian crafts. I didn't like being in The Girl Scouts, they were a rip off. You had to wear a dress and do all this girlie stuff, AND sell all those stupid cookies. I'd much rather be a Boy Scout. My coveting was interrupted by faint shouting, barely heard over the roaring of the river.

Mr. Wescott hurried out from behind his counter and ran towards the river. I didn't think the old man could move that fast. He crested the rise and stopped in his tracks. He stared for a second then spun around and ran back past me, towards Papa's truck. Flinging open the driver's side door he lunged across the seat and grapped the police radio handset.

Holy Cow! I thought, SOMETHING'S happenin'. I jumped up from my spot, and almost sprained my ankle coming off the porch. I ran straight for that rise on the river bank. Topping it, the first thing I noticed was one of the yellow rafts, upside down, about 50 yards downstream. It was caught up on some rocks and the rush of the water was ripping at the raft, trying to tear it free from the sharp angled rocks. A little bit to my left one of the adults was trying to help two kids get their footing on the slimey rocks. But they kept falling down, cutting their legs and their hands. The adult looked like he was close to tears, every time he'd pull one up the other would lose his footing and go down.

I glanced around frantically, looking for my grandfather. He was almost directly below me, standing chest-deep in the rushing whitewater, his face grim and strained. The last adult that came with the boys was also standing in the water. His back was to me, so I couldn't see his face. They seemed to be struggling with something, I couldn't quite make out what. Papa looked up and saw me standing above him. I'd never seen that look on my Papa's face before, he looked desparate. Suddenly, I was afraid.

The thing they were struggling with broke the surging surface of the water and I realized it was a boy. I knew in a second what was happening. The last raft of scouts had tipped over, and, somehow this boy had gotten some part of his body--I couldn't tell which from where I was standing, his shoulder, maybe--caught in the rocks. The current was moving so fast that he couldn't get back on his feet, or keep his head above water.

The man that was helping Papa lost his balance and slipped under, taking the boy with him. Papa reached over, his lips a white, bloodless slit. With all his might he pulled the man up, off the young boy. The man regained his footing, steadied himself against the river, and tried to help keep the boy's head up, so he could breath. I could see the boy's face. His eyes were huge, staring off at nothing, his lips a surprising shade of blue. One arm bobbed limply on the surface of the water.

When Mr. Wescott came up behind me and put his hand on my shoulder, I nearly fell headlong onto that poor boy.

"Go on," he said, then scurried down the bank to help. "Hap, Rescue's comin', they're on their way!"

I was still standing on the rise, my back to the river. A whole huddled troop of Boy Scouts stared at me blankly. I didn't know what to do. Should I just go sit down? Should I say something? Tell them that my Papa was here and he would make everything ok.

From far off through the trees I could hear the sirens. As I took a couple steps toward the scouts one of them burst into tears. They all turned away from me to stare at the crier.

A tribal police car, followed by an orange and white ambulance swung though the parking place, kicking up a cloud of dust, almost taking out what remained of the terrified boys in green. Doors flew open and men jumped out, running towards the river with blankets, tanks of oxygen, ropes and pulleys. People were yelling. Some guy with a coil of rope almost knocked me over as he ran past. I backed away toward the pick up, my chest feeling tight with fear. More official looking cars were pulling into the parking lot.

In the midst of all this my Papa suddenly appeared, soaking wet and still grim faced. His eyes met mine. Something in his face seemed to change. He started to move towards me, not even noticing when someone ran up and threw a blanket over his shoulders. He just kept right on walking straight at me. He put out his hand -- it seemed like he reached out a long way -- and cupped the back of my head. His hand seemed huge and for some reason this brought tears to my eyes. We just stood like that for a little while. I could hear voices all around me, scraps of different conversations:

"...water's just too strong..."

"...Where's the Troop Leader?"

"...they tried..."

"...no pulse..."

I looked up at Papa's weathered face. A sudden urge to throw myself into his arms hit me. His eyes welled up with tears. He blinked a couple of times, cleared his throat, and called to one of the tribal officers, who had been leaning against his cruiser.

"Billy..." he sniffled and wiped at his nose, "Will ya give my girl, here, a ride home to her ma?"

Billy, eagerly shook his head yes. He opened the car door for me and after I climbed in he shut it firmly. He and Papa exchanged a few words I couldn't hear because the window was rolled up. I rolled it down and half leaned out, watching my Papa. As the car pulled away I leaned out a little further and called loudly, so he could hear me,

"Papa, I love you."

Papa raised his hand. His lips moved. Then he turned away quickly. But I knew what his mouth said. It said: I love you.

As the patrol car pulled down the dirt avenue of pine trees I rolled up the window and sat back, watching the deep green forest slip past.

"So, how's your ma?" Billy asked me. I shrugged my shoulders, my eyes on the trees. I thought about my Papa.

MILLIE

I used to watch Millie - that was what they called her, since she wasn't allowed to use her real name at the boarding school - through the gate of the fence that separated the girl's playground from the boy's side. Millie was the nun's favorite. She was always neatly dressed, she knew her prayers and was always obedient. If someone fell during recess, Millie was always right there to tend to their needs and comfort the tears. She was 16, a good girl, who would pretend she wasn't aware of me or my long looks through the gate.

The nuns hated me. I would not forget who I was, my language or even my true name. I was named after my father, Wash-in-a-watok, the Concerned One. The nuns tried to tell me my name was Joseph White. Whenever they called on me to recite I'd sneer at them, cursing them in the language of my parents. The nuns would beat me, not because of what I said - they didn't speak Menominee, but because I didn't say it in their English.

It was during one of these beatings I knew Millie would be my wife. I had called Sister Mary George "the daughter of a bitch dog in heat." - in Menominee. She grabbed me by my hair and hauled me out of my seat with one hand, while she whipped me with her pointing stick in the other. The more I tried to struggle away from her the harder she hit me. The sister wanted me to cry out, beg her for mercy. I would have sooner bitten off my tongue than let a whimper escape my lips. The world darkened, my mind seemed to be floating away from me. Sister kept hitting.

I became aware of someone yelling.

"Stop, Sister!! Please! Stop!"

At first I thought it was me that was begging and I was ashamed. But then Sister Mary George did stop. When I could open my eyes I saw that Millie had put herself between me and the sister's rod. The nun stared at Millie in amazement, not believing such a good Christian girl would interfere with God's will. I took advantage of the sister's lapse and struggled to my feet.

"Millie, " Sister Mary George said in a warning tone. "Go back to your seat."

Millie shook her head.

"Millie, " sister said again. "Go to your seat or you will get a taste also." She held the stick up, waving it in Millie's face. Millie just stood there, eyes wide, cheeks flushed with color. Sister George cracked her high on the shoulder. Millie cried out. Without thinking I stepped forward and pushed the sister. She flew backwards, landing on her rear. The swirling black skirts tangling between her knobby stockinged knees. The nun raised herself up onto her elbows and begin to scream.

Millie shoved me towards the door.

"Go, Joseph!" She said in her stilted Menominee. "Don't come back."

The nuns decided I was "incorrigible." It didn't matter, by that time I was old enough to get a job. Millie's father hired me on as a lumberjack. He was foreman of the crew and knew I was hardworking, that I could support a wife. I told him I'd be good to her, I'd never hit her or let her want for anything. We both knew if Millie married me she wouldn't have to go back to the boarding school. Millie's father held out his hand for me to shake.

"I'd be glad to have you as a son-in-law. 'Course Millie's the one that's gotta decide."

I shook his hand, smiling. I already knew what his daughter would say. She would marry me.

When Millie came home for Christmas, I was there with a pair of warm winter boots, a bearskin robe and a small gold band. When I asked Millie she smiled up at me with shining eyes.

We were married the day after Christmas. I took her by the school to gather her things and say her goodbyes.

When the nuns saw her coming up the walk, they came flapping down the steps like a mob of angry crows. I could see Millie as they circled around her, pleading with her to come to her senses. She stood in the middle as the sisters cawed and pecked. Her hands folded together, her head slightly bent to hide the happy little smile that played across her lips. The nuns ushered her towards the door. Suddenly, I didn't want my wife setting foot in that damned place. Maybe the nuns would work their evil magic on her and she'd forget all about me, our little cabin, the band of gold. Then the nuns would marry her off to some one they thought more deserving. Some white farmer who would scoff at Millie and treat her like a pack animal.

"Millie!" I called as I jumped out of the sled. I hurried up to her. The sisters wouldn't let me through. The daughter of the bitch dog turned to Millie and took her hands. "Come with us, dear. Don't you realize this...heathen wants to make a squaw out of you?"

My wife looked up at the nun,
"No, Sister." She said gently, "not a squaw. He wants me to be Millie Washinawatok."
At this the nuns gabbled and sighed, knowing in their hearts she was lost to them. They parted ranks.

Millie stepped past them and took my hand.

RHINESTONE COWGIRL

You stupid bitch! those were the last words I heard before I slammed the phone down. I tore the blue floral wall paper from the boarders of the wall. I guess it was violent, but for me it was like Sunday church bells calling me to redemption through vengeance as I zig-zagged through the apartment. That's the only way I knew to clean my slate and state of mind, especially since he took off with my two-thousand dollar computer and drained our seventy-five hundred joint check account. It didn't occur to me that he was cheating with the waitress in a local restaurant and like my pop said, "Lawyers don't marry waitresses." I thought I was safe. Maybe that's where I went wrong.

Syngen was a lawyer, the only Indian lawyer I knew and met at Cornell University. He was a real sweetheart. He bought me enough rose pattern material to cover the concrete wall of my dormitory room. Later, he would say I was special like that. But it didn't last long. One year in the relationship and one bunch of carnations three months early for our anniversary, drew me into a cardboard box. He said it was his job, late nights reading and his daily workout routine, made him too tired for sex and conversation. He even pushed me into casual dating with Paul, my colleague, and if I knew where I would be today, I would be dining in restaurants and licking ice cream cones for lunch.

But here I am in Yvonne's apartment, a pillow in her forest green couch for the last week and a half. "You only live once," Donna , twice divorced and on a rebound, would say before exploiting her latest man. If I were smarter, I would probably be like her, living with every venereal disease in the book, and turning every Tom Dick and Harry looking for the gem perfect for my ring. That's the last thing I want. Besides, hemorrhoids are bad enough. Thirty -five and divorced. God damned with no children and no money.

Did I forget to mention, Syngen was my boss, "Out with the old, and in with the new," that was his motto. Every spring we shopped for new career clothes, he bought three piece suits and I the modest and conservative dress suit in all colors. He said he liked me like that, professional and clean, unlike the slap suit of a waitress but I guess I can't blame him.

I became his pretty little wife, a half human shell. I forgot my own depth and personal freedom and lived in his silver water. I saw green for go when it was yellow and flew through the chutes anyway, hoping to get first prize.

Funny. This must be the season for divorce, even the weather has been strange. Yesterday the news said masses of seals were dying off the coast. The problem has not been identified. Julie, the new girl upstairs from Yvonne, has been divorced three months, said her ol' man was screwing hookers in the street then divorced her for sleeping with another woman. Crazy. I guess she thought they had an understanding. Get it in writing, sign the dotted line, that's what I say. Even on receipts, if you pay one brass cent, sign for it; don't let it slip you by.

Slipping by, that just about sums it up. Charlotte, separated over a year, two children, a dog and mortgage payments, let it slip by. She's in prison now. Shot the son-of-a-bitch dead and dragged his body down to the basement before her kids got back from the late night show. Said she was fed up and wanted a new life. She's got one now plus a new number to sign along with her social security. Gone Hysterical! That's where marriage gets you. Braces an apron around you loaded with dynamite and some matches. See if you have the balls or the scars to carry the load. Hasta-la-vista baby. What happened to the good ol' days.

My parents married 65 years, still nagging and poking with canes. Said it takes tons of kisses and several pounds of insults, left-hand jabs, upper-cuts and diabolic minds with the forgiveness of a dove. Just a whole lotta pain for survival. But not even marriage is a bless-ed sitcom. Their advice to me, "Dust yourself off and get back on that horse. Just a rhinestone cowgirl who needed a good kick in the head."

JIMMY RED DOG

Jimmy Red Dog sat outside of his favorite strip joint. The neon lights still flashed as the New Mexico sun began to peep over the horizon. The sun's light blazed into Jimmy's bloodshot eyes. He sat on the sidewalk searching for his $2.99 K-mart-special sunglasses. His red flannel shirt was torn from a fight he was in hours ago. Jimmy had dried blood on his blue Levi jeans and on his swollen upper lip. "It wasn't my fuckin' fault," he silently said to himself while still searching for his shades. Jimmy looked again in his right shirt pocket finding a joint at the bottom. He leaned back on his bruised elbows and lit the joint. Jimmy toked on it like it was his last. The sweet smoke calmed and relaxed him like a mother cradling her new-born baby. His mind was at ease once again.

"Last night was totally insane," Jimmy thought to himself as he sat on the sidewalk and waited for his cab. Jimmy could see the yellow car in the distance and scrambled to his feet counting how much cash he had left. As the cab shrieked to a halt, Jimmy could smell the exhaust from the muffler and gagged. Jimmy hopped into the backseat, "Take me to the local jail!" he told the cab driver, who was wearing a white turban on top of his head.

The cab driver leaned back, "Marlboro? Looks as if you could use a hospital." Jimmy grabbed the cigarette and took a look at himself in the rear-view mirror. He had no idea how bad he looked, and after looking at himself he could understand why the cabby said such a thing. "Just take me to the local jail!" Jimmy lit the cigarette and began wondering how Sharon was doing.

Sharon Whitecrow sat on a steel cot. Her head was resting on her knees, tears rolled down her face. Sharon was Jimmy's girlfriend at the time, and because of him she sat incarcerated. "How could I have been that stupid?," she whispered to herself. Sharon began thinking about the night before when Jimmy went to meet her...

Jimmy walked into the dorm lobby of the Institute of American Indian Arts. He often went there to meet Sharon. Jimmy was wishing something good was going to happen that night. Just about every weekend Sharon and Jimmy would go to his favorite strip joint. Sharon didn't mind, she loved Jimmy and would do just about anything for him.

Sharon came out of the TV room to meet him. Jimmy already held the pool stick in his hand ready to hussle anyone who was willing to try to beat him. Sharon leaned against the wall, pushed back her long dark hair. She liked to watch "her man" play pool. He looked so strong, so in control just like he was in bed.

Jimmy played five games, undefeated. He collected his fifty bucks and told Sharon to get ready. They both went into her dorm room. She began to change, but never finished because Jimmy began to caress her body. Jimmy then unbuckled his pants and ripped off Sharon's panties, slammed her against the wall and began thrusting into her.

An hour later they were off to "Cheeks" where "they tease to please." Sharon sat down at the bar when Jimmy went over to some guy to score some crack. When Jimmy returned, Sharon could tell he scored because of the unnatural way he was smiling. Jimmy sat down next to Sharon, ordered himself a Bud and two Southern Comfort shots for her. He leaned over and whispered into Sharon's ear, "I'm going to get you fucked up tonight!'

Sharon was hesitant to go with him back to the car. She had watched him crack it, hundreds of times before but she had never done it herself. She knew how crazy Jimmy got on that shit and she wasn't about to do it herself. Jimmy got his pipe out from underneath the seat of his 1969 Thunderbird. "I don't want to do that shit, Jimmy. I'm uneasy about the thing." Sharon told him. Jimmy shot her a steamy look and with that look she knew she had no choice. Jimmy lit and guided the pipe to Sharon's mouth for her first hit.

Not even a minute went by when she jumped out of the car throwing up uncontrollably. The vomit hit the parking lot pavement with such force that it splattered back into her face. The smell was so bad that Sharon began to puke even more.

When Sharon regained her posture they both went back into the bar. Sharon went right to the ladies room while Jimmy went to order more drinks. In the bathroom Sharon washed her face and also washed out the chunks of vomit in her hair. She stood there in front of the 12" X 8" scum infested mirror looking at herself while feeling around in her purple leather purse for her perfume. Sharon was feeling pretty damn good despite the chunks still in her hair and the strong odor of her clothing.

After about fifteen minutes, Jimmy was on his fourth Bud and getting really impatient, " What the fuck is that damn bitch doing, taking so long!" Finally, Sharon came strolling out, her long damp hair bounced with every step she took. As she sat down, Jimmy began, "What the fuck were you taking so long for? Christ sakes, woman." Sharon was sitting there watching Jimmy's lips move but wasn't hearing a word. Sharon was too busy listening to the song on the jukebox, "I Love Rock & Roll," by Joan Jett. In the middle of Jimmy's lecture, Sharon bursts out laughing at him. She was laughing so hysterically that Jimmy stood up and was about to slap her when the bouncer came over to the table to see what was going on.

As soon as the bouncer got to the table, Sharon jumped up on the top of the table with a beer bottle in her left hand and smashed it over the six-foot, 239 pound bouncer's head. Then she hopped on his back and began punching him. It all happened so fast that Jimmy and everyone else in the bar didn't know what the hell was going on. Jimmy went to grab Sharon, but she kicked him in the mouth and he fell to the floor. The next thing Jimmy knew, he was in a middle of a bar brawl.

The bouncer, after recovering from the hit on the head, grabbed Sharon who was still clutched around his neck punching him, threw her across the room. Sharon landed square in the middle of a table, she hit her head on a glass ashtray, knocking her out. Sharon woke up in jail.

Sharon decided to lay down, her head was still throbbing. "That's all I remember," she thought to herself. "I wonder what Jimmy's doing?," she thought just as the guard went and opened the steel door, entered her cell. "You have a visitor, come with me."

Sharon walked into the corridor, Jimmy sat with his head down on the opposite side of the plexiglass. Sharon sat down on the gray folding chair and picked up the phone. Jimmy did the same. Before any one of them said anything, Sharon burst into tears. Jimmy sat and listened to her sobbing. Finally, Jimmy said, "Sharon will you shut up, your giving me a fuckin' headache!" Sharon stopped her crying, "I love you, Jimmy." Jimmy didn't say anything because he was disgusted. "I should have just broke up with her yesterday, things happened," Jimmy thought to himself. Jimmy cleared his throat, "I just came to tell you good-bye, it's over." He stood up, turned and was gone.

Sharon eyes filled with hot angry tears and she bit her lip so hard it began to bleed. Her hand was clutched onto the phone so tight there was white in her knuckles. Her throat ached and even to breathe would hurt. Then without even thinking she jumped up, grabbed the gun out of the guard's holster and placed the gun to her head. A second later, she laid on the white tiled floor with her own blood splattered on the wall beside her.

SALMON HAVE TO DREAM TOO, FREDDY

Hey, how's it going?

How was your summer?

Mine was okay. We just got back from my aunt's last week.

My sister, she just gets weirder and weirder. You see, my aunt has a pool with a slide and a diving board. My sister lived in that thing all summer. I mean, as soon as she got there, she wanted to jump in the pool. When she finally did get in, she jumped in on the deep side. Everyone got scared. Mom about had a cow. My sister just swam underwater until she got to the shallow side. She came up out of the water smiling. They got mad at her and told her not to do that again.

Now she wants to be a swimmer. She says she wants to swim the Irish Channel.

I'm sure she means the English Channel. She'd sometimes say she was a mermaid. Other days she was a dolphin, a shark, or some other kind of water animal. I swear to God, she's so goofy. I don't remember being that weird as a kid. Remember last year, she wanted to be a fire fighter? She damn near burned down the tool shed. She said she was practicing so she can be prepared to put out a fire.

Yeah, and mom and dad encouraged her to act so goofy. One time she found an old white robe in the closet. She went around pretending to be a doctor. Then mom and dad bought her a toy doctor kit. She would put all of her dolls in bandages and shit. I felt sorry for that poor cat who had to be her patient. The little cat is scared to hell of her now.

Now she says her name is Irma Veronique. She won't ever answer to the name Destiny. She's always walking around wearing mom's jewelry and this big yellow hat on her head. Yesterday, she was trying to wear high heels and kept falling down. Mom and dad just laughed at her. I'm surprised she didn't twist her ankle or anything.

Now that I think of it, she was also a weird baby. She never wanted to take a bath. She would always find a way to escape and then she'd be running around the house naked while everyone chased her. When she was about two, we came back from the movies, and we still had some popcorn left in one of those big buckets. She got the popcorn, poured it all out on the living room rug, put the bucket on her head and started dancing around. I thought they were gonna yell at her or something. Instead, everyone was laughing. My dad got the camera out and started taking pictures of her. When she was about one-and-a-half, she used to always talk up a storm in her baby talk, and then she'd bust out laughing. Everyone would laugh with her, though they didn't know what the hell she was saying.

Now she keeps trying to talk mom and dad into buying her a swimming pool. She says she wants to practice for when she swims the Channel. Mom tells her they can't afford buying no swimming pool. They promised her that they'll take her to the lake as much as they can. Guess who has to watch her. She's already gone swimming four times since we've gotten back. When we go swimming, she makes me get in the lake with her and she pretends like we're at Sea World and I hold out my hand while she jumps up pretending like she's eating fish from my hand.

What am I doing now? Mom's buying Destiny ballerina stuff. Now she wants to dance.

Funny, huh? Yeah, I guess she's gonna be dancing across the water while swimming the English Channel. I swear, the girl is insane.

Oh, there they are. I guess I gotta go. What are you doing tomorrow?

Yeah. Well, I might come by and see you. Maybe we could play basketball. That's if I don't have to watch my sister.

Well, I gotta go. Check ya' later.

Oh, hi Destiny.

Excuse me. Irma.

What?

No. I don't want to.

herm. Okay. But I won't neigh.

All right, I'll gallop. Come on.

HIVE O CLOCK SHADOW

5:00 AM

Fork's eyes pried open as two trap doors to his real fiction, revealing his musky blue floor's carpet. He shivered reaching for his rope burned throat and glanced skyward, "Futobi-for."The Horned Larks are singing their "Love the morning" songs outside the sharked window, as he chokes, rocking from side to side on the floor's carpet. His hoarse voice is a short cry from the crypt, "Fu, shit yeah, that's it, oh yeah." He covers his face with a clammy blanket of hands. "Right now, right here, right now. Where's my medicine? Where? Is it, is it. I'm going to find out, and when I do I'll fuck all you, you bitchiah, oh. SHIT."

Squealing tires and the roar of gravel sounded almost real to Fork. "Crash," and the voice of glass's bending breath. His trailer lurched and jumped the blocks that held the flat wheels static. Fork hears every bowl, plate, and glass break three by three in the kitchen's belly, as his home slid across the red earth. A brown clay lamp trips onto the floor. The black round clock saying five o'five falls violently from the wall next to Fork's head and danced to the floor's carpet like a spinning penny. The stillness is a snow fall in the dead of winter. It is good.

Fork lies very still, as not to brake the fragile snow fall. Then heaved dry in the fortune that was turning in his guts. The mind of his possession was churning to black oil curd. "What you cannot be, I cannot be. This, that whore all. He." This soothed the lithe passion of his wounded breath for an instant and he rubbed his throat once again. "Me? Me. Fuck. As you are." The cool of the damp living room floor's carpet hung round his neck like a foul stinkbug loin.

The light of a new day shone the dust flakes off the brisk morning air's bite. "Face another one. More beating of my body's filth. More panting of the stink I long to dismiss. Aaah. I decay yet again. Why not another? Why not? Feast. But I will spare the world no kindness." Fork winced as he tries to rise on his hands and knees and crumpled back to the floor's carpet. "Ha, ha, ha. Fork. You're going to die someday, damn it." He tries to get up once again when the trailer shifted. The entertainment system leaned and fell. The television set and all else landed on the back of his head. The birds sing praise for their lives in the maple.

6:00 AM

Fork awoke with an Ass bite in the back of his skull. "Oooooh, man." He positions his arms and pushes up. Pain, inhuman, and potency flung the entertainment system up where gravity broke it on Fork's catwalk spine. "Ooooh, man. That's it. We're having too much fun now." Fork's realm lurches him to his feet. He stumbles barefoot about his tilted fun house kingdom; Fork pushes through his ruins to the restroom.

He tries the light switch, "Don't work eh." Fork lashes out his manhood and without aiming "aaah." He reaches to flush, "Looks like You ate something, last night at least." He moves, "Chunky, chunky, chunky is a good sign."

Fork's dark reflection inspects every handsome scar as he tries to wash his hands. White lint and grass freckle his crue-top from the binge days past. Oddly, Fork looks to the left. "The crapper doesn't work," and he dries his thirsty hands on his 505 jeans. He looks back at his estranged features, "What has happened?" He scratches under his right eye. "You will live today, it seems. Yes. Find the reason for today then. A sound thought, you must act upon. But why? It seems you are just meant to be. Then will the wind take you with the red leaves of autumn this day. Good then." Fork's image grins back at him, then turns into a look, "Quit talking to them, ah ... us, I mean, yourself, fool. Let's go."

He prods through the rubble once more and strides out the door, "Thud." Red mud fountains up from ground zero. Spraying the walls of the trailer like blood in a bag. On his face, the stairs are four feet away. Fork lifts his cadaver out the red earth from where he comes.

Standing draped in mud, Fork rips off his T-shirt. He sniffs at the perfumed air of gasoline's potential. Fork walks on to find Joe's Ford is deep throating his kitchen. "Joe, you dumb slut." There is no answer but the tick of the tank. Fork coils to the car door, "What do you want, damn it?"

Joe casually turns his head without emotion. Fork tries the door, "Get out of there, you dicked up my house, damn it."

Joe gives Fork a halfhearted grin, and methodically faces forward. Joe's smile is complete with tears running down his high cheek bones. He slides a Colt magnum from his blue windbreaker and systematically palces it to his temple.

Fork's eyes flash and burn as he putshis fist through the window. The gun makes no noise. Muffled by flesh offerings. Only shards of skull and pie sound of brain can be heard, as Fork is assaulted by shrapnel.

Fork blinks, looking through the tiled sauce cavern that is Joe. He tastes the iron of Joe, and he spits and coughs until there's no more red. "Damn you, drunk bastard, you slut." He smacks his chops and crinkles his dark nose. "What will become?" Time is soft down and comforting in the slow breeze that dries the brown crust on Fork's face as he stands shivering. "You dumb shit. My fire is smoked."

7:00 AM

He limps around his trailer to access the damages. The aluminum siding is torn and is paper. Half of the once green yard is either a calm glass or a bloody muck. "It seems your pipes are toast as well."

The chill in death jogged down Fork's bruised spin. Tyoki, his faithful German shepherd, lay crushed after the wheel. "No, not you. Anyone but you." Fork sank before his old friend's remains and pets his head, scratches behind the ears and smoothes out Tyogi's damp fur. "Good morning, good night, have a bone that is your own, and that is what reality bites."

Fork crumbles to the green blades. Slumped over himself like a raw slab of blooded beef, he stares at a dandelion. Its yellow petals mimic wasp wings in the cool early morning breeze. The light of the sun did not blink or yawn, as it awoke on this woeful stage called the State of New York. The dandelion begins to blur in Fork's vision. A warm trail walks from his eyes to his lips. It tastes warm, salty, and sweet at first, but soon turns into the metallic sips of weeping.

His ass is wet when he rises. He reaches for his wallet and extracts a "J" as the sweet smell of natural gas hits his smeller. He lights a match, then his "J." His house engulfs the flames and is the tomb of two as Fork walks down the dirt road in his quest for breakfast.

THE KING

Smoke billowed out the chimney, the lights danced to the music of a handgame in full swing. The moon was full and bright. We watched from the main house window; red dots outside where the men took long drags of their cigarettes, figures dancing to a rhythmic beat inside the cabin.

We did this every Saturday or so it seemed. Dee pushed the window up so we could hear it all. Faye would pinch her nose and sing real loud as she copied the older women sing. Then we all would hide.

"Ah shut up you brats! I'm calling your folks," uncle IK would laugh. He dressed western, he pushed his coat back as though he were ready for a gun fight, then he walked with his thumbs in his front pockets. All the men in those days dressed like cowboys. we knew IK though, his belly popped over his pants and in the shadows, he looked like Alfred Hitchcock.

"He acts so handsome, who would want to kiss him?" Dee says as she wrinkles her nose.

"Well, ah, your auntie does! An' when you grow up, you'll probably marry his son!" Faye laughed and ran around the chair.

That certain night, we were watching the Ed Sullivan Show. Our family was one of the first families to have black and white television. Well, what was different, was this particular music. Our curiosity got the best of us, we pushed each other and took off running. We couldn't believe our eyes. It was the first time we'd seen Elvis! Sliding down together, side to side like a burnt down candle, our hearts flamed together like a bon fire. Our pupils dilated and mouths wide open. Our lives changed there.

"Oh geez, do you think he likes Indians?" I looked into the mirror and smiled."An' do you think he would come to Wyoming?"

The man in the moon smiled down at me, I jerked the curtain shut. My mind wandered back to his eyes and back to those pouty lips of his. Elvis, I thought.

"No he's too rich. He was in Hawaii singing, not in Wyoming. That bus ticket must of cost him at least $50.00! My Auntie watches him all the time." Dee says as she yawns long and hard. Quietly she sits straight on the edge of the chair with her legs crossed, then leans over to get a cigarette butt and pretends to smoke.

The door opens fast as Mom flips on the light switch and peeks into the living room. Behind her trails dad counting his money. On paydays, everyone would start betting with money. Any other time they only played for junk.

"What are you all doing up? It's late! and who are you watching?" Mom squints her eyes at the TV, " Don't cho be watching that Elvis, He dances too nasty! An, where'd you put that switch JR?"

She always chased us to bed with that switch, but never really hit us. Well a time or two; when we put the car in reverse and left Baby Shay in there. It didn't mess the car up and Shay was okay. Besides Grandpa was always fixin' fences and he didn't mind fixing the fence. Yeah, come to think of it, we got switchin's as much as we had fun.

Before that revaluating night, Brian would sit by me everyday during lunch. We were in the 1st grade, he also sat by me in class. We would make Nellie's ringlets bounce hard and blame it on Kevin when she looked back at us. Our class smelt of plastic and new books. Brian would save me a place in line, smiling so hard as he motioned for me. But, when Dee and Faye were with me, he wouldn't let us have cuts.

"That's okay. Mame doesn't like you anymore. She likes an older man." Dee stood with her nose pointing to the air, after Brian just rejected our little gang.

Dee spilled the beans! Punching her in the stomach, her laugh was like a machine gun. The laugh echoed 'til Mame grabbed her hair and twisted it till she hollered.

"Okay, okay! I won't tell anyone that you like Elvis." Dee ran to the side and looked at Mame and Faye. "I'm sorry, I'm your best friend, you know I wouldn't tell anyone who you like.

The cafeteria was still empty, the higher grades would arrive later. Looking around the room, I saw a sad face looking and then turning away. I thought of all the bubblegum and jawbreakers, he used to give me. Where do I sit in class now? Now he'll like Nellie and her ringlets. He was the best dressed cowboy in class and he made his hair flip with that greasy stuff Brylcream.

Faye came to my rescue with a picture."The lady over there, who works in the library gave this to you." Faye puts her arm around my shoulder. We both outlined his face with our fingers, then took turns kissing the picture. The weather was getting colder, Faye put the picture in the pocket inside her coat and hugged herself

We stood together in the cool night breeze, using bits of dried weeds as fake cigarettes and pretending to smoke. Our breath puffed out like smoke, like exhaling cigarette smoke. Mom made us wait outside while the men smoked and left for the tipi. It was cool, to smell the smoke and cedar. After everyone was situated in the tipi, we got to go in the house. The living room was warm, we grabbed ourselves a donut and sat by our babysitter.

"Elvis was in a movie with a little Chinese girl, did you know that? I think it was Blue Hawaii." Hatty, the babysitter was saying, "She looked like an Indian girl, it could of been you!" she smiled at us.

Hatty, she used to fix her hair in a bubble and put on long false eyelashes. I remember she was a tiny lady, in a year of two, we would all be as tall as her. Sometimes she would bring her records of Diana Ross and the Supremes and we'd all dance. But of course, not this night, we were supposed to be quiet.

"If we ran away, do you think we could find Elvis's house? I don't think he would be mad. Besides I heard he was an Indian, is he? eyebrows raised with wonder.

We followed Elvis's singing career, as we grew along with him. My friends and I met when ever we could. Dee was loud and boisterous, if you didn't already figure this out.She was so skinny and tall, yeah, maybe she was pretty. She got on my nerves a lot, but always managed to hang by me. When we would try to ditch her at a pow-wow or something, my mom would holler at us.

"She's your first cousin, be nice to her. Her dad and your dad are brothers," Mom reminded us constantly. My mom was always keeping peace, especially in our families. She never teases us of the boys we talked about. If she heard anything of Elvis she would let us in on it. I remember on the news report in our little town, they mentioned "Elvis would be stopping in at our Airport." We were so hyper, but we also knew that the roads were packed with snow. The road up to the airport was very steep, so we kept our mouths shut.

My mom and Auntie checked us out of school, they were being very mysterious. We wondered if it were something bad.

"We're going to the airport,why?" Dee leaned over the seat. We were so baffled: it never occurred to us that we were going to see Elvis.

The closer we got, cars and trucks were parked along the road. White ladies dressed up nice like they were going to church, could care less that they walked on the side of the muddy roads. Farmers, with their suspenders and checkerboard shirts on, sat on top of their trucks. Mom, she's so cool! she parks right in the front of the reserved parking spot.

"I'm scared! What if he got all those letters we wrote to him. I don't want to go to Hawaii, don't you love me?" Leaning in the back seat and kicking the front seat enough to make the ladies' heads shake, I cried.

We stayed hiding in the car, Dee and I did. After what seemed hours, the people came out slowly with smiles on their faces. Teenage white boys wiggled on their ankles as they tried to imitate the King, another looked in the reflection of a car window and carefully combed his hair just like The King. Our mothers got in the car not saying a word, it was puzzling. They acted like they went to fill the car up with gas or something

As we parked at the grocery store parking lot in our dinky town, my father drove up. At the time he was a Game Warden for the tribe, so his winter green 4x4 truck drove up honking. He laughed and laughed pounding the hood of the car, as he walked our way.

'So you all seen Elvis! tee hee, I heard he was real hairy!" I knew there was something funny the way he laughed at mom when he said, "Your mom went to see Elvis the Chimp, at the airport," as he leaned in the window.

"We were just taking the girls to see him, you know

how they like everything about Elvis." as she took a drag and blew the smoke in his face. Mom always looked with halfway opened eyes when she didn't want to admit she was wrong.

We kept our pride knowing we weren't fooled by the Elvis imposter. Imagine that, a stinky hairy monkey that could care less if his skinny hairy butt showed. As the snow melted, my friends were slowly leaving; one went to Denver, another family went on relocation to California. I watched American Bandstand alone, I don't remember seeing Elvis on there either. I didn't feel like getting new friends, I had enough sisters.

Walking around the Sundance grounds one summer, I heard thunderous hoof beats behind me. The dust raced on past me as the horse rider stopped by me. I looked up and saw a grown familiar face, as he smiled.

"Do you still like Elvis? Don't you know this is the best looking Indian guy's face you'll see?" he sits straight on his horse as if he were in a parade, "I still like you, as long as you don't compare me to that old man." I put one foot in the stirrup and he pulled me onto the back of the horse. It was hot and dusty, we had to stay off the main road. A loud car drives by playing "A hunka hunka burning love...", it was my old pals.

"Now if you leave or even wave, I'm not going to give you another chance." Smiling as he threw rocks into the ditch. We stopped there for his horse to cool off.

While babysitting, I lay on top of the old pump house roof that Dee, Faye and I would play on. My little niece and her friends were screaming and laughing, I kept falling in and out of boredom. I remembered Elvis, I could only picture his face as a young man even though he was getting older. I looked in a small mirror then up in the sky, I heard he got married. An' I hear his new bride was so young! She wasn't even of age, so, maybe there was a chance. If only we ran away like we wanted to. Feeling a stare, the little girls looked at me like I was crazy.

I grew taller and grew in other places, I kinda realized how silly it was to worship Elvis like he were perfect. In the 70's everyone was into drugs, especially Elvis. His suits of gemstones, capes and bigbells, couldn't cover that weight he had accumulated. I felt sorry for him the more I seen him. His hair would be pasted with sweat, even under all the hairspray. I could see him puffing with every breath just to say, "Thank you, Thank you very much."

I thought of when I first saw him way back then, it was his voice that kept him rocking. In my thoughts, I still see his pretty face and those pouty lips. I also came to realize, he is not an Indian or I would of seen plenty of Indian guys lookin' like that. Sadly, Elvis's shadow looks like the Alfred Hitchcock character I once joked about.

NOTHIN' SACRED

"SHUT UP! SHUT THE FUCK UP!!!" The screen door slammed against the house. Tammy stomped through the front door with Pete yelling behind her.

She stopped out on their dead lawn. Shriveled flowers, a broken fence, and old toys scattered all over what used to be her pride and joy. Tammy spit the blood out of her mouth onto the grass, then wiped her face with her shirt. "You fuckin' bastard! I HATE YOU!!....You hear me?!" She spit again, "YOU AIN'T SHIT!"

Tammy looked around then reached down and picked her son's bat up off the dead grass. She could hear Pete's footsteps marching toward the door. His head popped out then he flung the screen door open, bashing it up against the side of the house. All 6'2", 230 lbs. of him filled up the doorway except for the corners where the t.v.'s light flickered through. "Tammy, please just go to bed," he said in a calm tone. He stepped out onto the porch, "just go lay down until you sober up."

Tammy gripped the bat, "No, I don't have to do shit, you fuckin' asshole!" Tammy's loud voice could be heard all over town. As the sun's last light peered over the western hills, blinds began to open, televisions turned down, and people came out of their houses to get a better look.

Feeling the burn of public gaze, Pete kept his cool and tried to take control of the situation, the way the community would want him to. "Look honey, just come inside, we can talk this over." Pete put on his Million Dolllar Smile, "please, Honey?"

Tammy's eyes nearly popped out of her head. *Honey?* she thought. The only time Tammy Wagner ever heard that word was when Pete was introducing her to bigshots at council meetings and conferences, or when his out-of-shape-ex-football-player-2-six-pack-and-a-donut-body rolled off after a quickie. Beauracrats made her sick, and being married to one made life that much harder.

"Fuck you!" she yelled. Pete just laughed it off, the Million Dollar Smile in full force.

"Please, baby, just come inside."

Tammy swung at the word "baby." Pete was trying

113

his systematic-beaurocratic approach that years of working for the BIA had taught him. Too bad for him those lines only worked on Congressmen, and white women who eat up Indian men with long hair and Mystic Warrior tendencies.

"What? Oh, I'm sorry, am I embarrassing you?" Tammy apologized and returned a bloody smile. "Worried about what people will think?" Her smile grew, "Think I might ruin the great reputation of Council Member Peter Wagner?" The Million Dollar Smile went down to about a buck fifty. "Hey everybody look!" Tammy turned around to face the adoring public of the Tribe. "All you kids take a look at what a great leader is!" Her voice bounced off every house, seeped through every fence, and planted itself wherever it could. "When you grow up you should be just like this." Pete stood watching his wife, "Grow up and do this to your wife, spend half your money at the bar, and save the rest for the whorehouses!"

Pete ran up behind her and clamped his hand over her mouth, his other arm went around her body. The two began struggling. Tammy bit his hand and made Pete pull it back. Then she jammed the bat up under her crotch into Pete's testicles. He dropped to the ground.

"See this lip?!" Tammy backed up holding the bat, "You did this. Good ole' Pete Wagner, you son of a bitch!" As Pete rolled on the ground trying to pull his jewels out of his stomach, sirens blared in the distance.

The screen door creaked open and in the doorway stood Little Debbie watching her parents. Pete noticed her right away.

"Go in the house baby." He turned away so she couldn't see his eyes "Daddy will be in a little bit, okay." Tammy turned and looked at her too.

"Yeah, baby go on in the house and watch your brother, okay?" She said as she hid the bat behind her back. Tammy put on a smile for her 'angel' and tried to hide the bat further behind her back, "Mommy will be in a little bit." Debbie gazed the two over, and went inside.

Her little brother Marcus was sleeping on the couch.

Debbie turned the volume up to drown out her parents dramatic performance. After seven years of it, it all sounded the same.

Tammy heard the cops coming. A quick thought about grabbing the kids and taking off in the car passed through her mind, then it died with the grass, as the lights and sirens rounded the block and came up into sight.

The sun ducked behind the dusty hills of the desert and left pink and blue traces in the sky. Pete lay on his side, recovering.

"See what you did..." he mumbled, "... stupid bitch.".

Tammy spun around, "I FUCKIN' HATE YOU!" she screamed as she swung down at her husband. Pete caught the bat and jerked it forward throwing her off balance. Tammy flipped over off the grass, and into the dirt. The cops pulled into the yard. Pete threw the bat and jumped up. Tammy scrambled up off the dirt to her feet. More out of instinct than anger, Pete followed up with a right cross to her face and a left uppercut to her jaw that released the bat from her hand and sent her to the ground, dazed. Pete stood above her looking at his hands in shock, wondering, if he'd just did what he did. Tammy gained her senses and scrambled for the bat. Pete made a quick step and kicked it away. Tammy sprung up and punched him in the gut, knocking out his wind. Pete leaned forward trying to catch his breath.

All eyes fixed on the bout, some rooted for Tammy on the inside, while others spoke outloud how much she deserved it. Tammy sent a kick that blew out Pete's bad knee. He fell to the ground, breathless, holding his leg. Tammy walked off the lawn and picked up the bat, as she did Pete shook his head clear, but stayed on the ground, covering up as Tammy came running at him cocking back to swing. Just as she was about to, Pete leaped off the ground and planted a straight right that splattered blood all over. The punch sent Tammy flying back and Pete lost his one legged balance and collapsed to the ground. As the two lay there, bloody and unconscious, curtains slid shut and lights came back on.

KNUCKLES & FIST

Some had heard, some had seen. It was Nate, he had been picked by Woolie Wil. Once the talk caught wind, it spread through the playground. Some said it happened over by the monkey bars. Others had it going on by the bathrooms. Neither were their usual hangout.

Woolie Wil usually hung by the courts. Muscling up kids for lunch money were his recess activites, while Nate's stomping grounds were playing kickball by the boy's bathroom. They were two seemingly unopposing forces, which were brought together by a tragic mixture of dirt and cream.

From what was going around, Nate got hold of one of Matty James' inside pitches and launched it over to the big kid's side of the playground. The ball took a bounce of a third grader, then sped towards the courts. Woolie Wil was counting his daily hustle while digging in his lunch when it knocked one of his cupcakes on the ground. Time froze as the cup cake free-falled to the ground, hit the dirt, and split open exposing the delicate creamy insides. As the pastry's last moments of freshness dwindled, Woolie Wil looked on, helpless.

Swings stopped swinging, basketball' stopped bouncing, and kids kissing by the monkey bars sucked their tongues back in to pay respect to the fallen.

It was common knowledge Woolie Wil loved his cupcakes. Everyday two things were sure to be with the hefty seventh grader: a grimmace and a sack lunch. Stomping through the hall, his left hand held the paper sack, daily contents: two Albertson ham and cheese sandwiches, two cokes, and three cupcakes..respectively., In his right was held the power to protect it.

Fear forced people to the side when they caught sight of the sack. When he strode down the hall, Woolie Will's fingers looked like over cooked sausages that clinched tight the nameless and solitary sack.   His was the only one in the whole school that didn't have a name on it. This characteristic told would-be-thieves and malnourished, underpaid faculty, the risk they took dare they violate its contents.

Some had, and along with one of the deluxe sandwiches came a fat fist to help wash it down. As a fourth grader, it was rumored that Woolie Wil had taken on the Old Principal Christenson for sneaking a bite from one of his sandwiches. As it went, Woolie Wil was pastor to the Hostess gods, with double chins and sweaty rolls to show his faith.

On the flip side stood Nate Numaga. A fourth grader with some size and an addiction to kickball. Standing four feet, six inches he'd been a kickball legend since second grade, when he stepped up to Johnny Farmer, formidable but aging eighth grader, and put three of his pitches over the fence. Never to be outdone on the field, Nate was skilled at the art of defense. He caught weak flyballs in the backfield, ran them in to cover second, and put the lights out on any greedy soul brave enough to attempt a stolen base.

Unmerciful but equal, even girls who braved onto the field knew the risks. On one lunch recess last year folks still recall the time Suzy Winnemucca, fifth grade "tomboy", decided to jump in. Little Herbie Vasquez was on third and Big Chow led off second. Underestimating her power, Nate sent a "lady-guy"pitch down the pipe and she launched it out to left field towards the 'goat heads.' Chris "Crisco" Walker made the attempt. It bounced off his chest then back up into the air. Suzy made first and gunned towards second. Herbie made the score and Big Chow huffed with all his might to third. Suzy rounded second and kept going. Crisco finally got hold of the ball and lobbed it off to Nate, who was waiting between second and third. Tempting maim, Suzy decided to take the chance and go for it. With Big Chow three-quarters of the way to home. Nate gave up on the run and set his sights set on the runner. As Suzy crossed midway through to third she saw Nate winding back the ball. She hesitated for a second and that gave Nate all he needed. As the fear came to Suzy's face, Nate Numaga locked, loaded, and launched on his prey.

All anybody could do was watch the red streak head for the helpless, frightened face. Younger kids turned away, as the hit took her off her feet and down on the hot, unforgiving pavement. Some say she was out cold before she even hit the ground. As she lay there unconscious, Big Chow finally made it in.   Little Herbie Vasquez rushed to get help while Big Herbie checked her vitals.

It was a gruesome sight, but one that stood as a fine example of what fair really is.

The field, the ball, even the game belonged to Nate. Who watched with unblinking eyes as Mr. Burselli and Mrs. Jones came on the scene to revive the fallen.

Most just remember the boy just standing there holding the ball, on the field, waiting for the game to go on.

INTRO TO LAST OF THE OLD BASTARDS

Thinking back to home and growing up, I remember "The Courts." Set down on the north end of the Natchez School playground, this was the chapel of my childhood.

It's not much to look at today. Two slabs of pavement with three hoops on each side is all you see from the highway that passes right in front of the school. When you step into the school yards, you'll find shards of glass scattered all over, goathead weeds growing up through the cracks, and the occasional dead dog now and then.

On windy days, what's left of the chain nets still clank together. Battles won and lost on those courts run back and forth like sports reels on the six o' clock news for anybody that listens close enough.

Sneaker prints pushed deep into the pavement are covered by glass and weeds. One day they'll be discovered again. When the young uncover them, they'll see the petroglyphs telling stories of those who "ran" on that court back in the day. Records carved in poles also let the youngsters know that "Big Mike was here," " Gabe is a fag," and "Weylen sucks fat dick."

LAST OF THE OLD BASTARDS

A lot of people play basketball. People all over the world grab a ball after school or work then go out shooting in parks, schools, even jail. They'll play pick up for an hour or so then take off home.

For the most part it's just a game. You play until you're beat and/or too bruised up to go on, so you end up going home until the next game.

In some cases it goes deeper than that. Something more goes inside the game making it more than some part time hobby. That's something I never realized until later on in life. Now looking back, I see the impact the game really had.

I was brought up in the town of Wadsworth, Nevada. It's another dirt in the long list of dirt towns that sprinkle the entire state. It sits on the southwest corner of the Pyramid Lake Paiute Reservation. Elevation is around 4317ft. Wadsworth's population is a little over 2100. If you were to somehow get a bird's eye view, it would resemble a big birthday cake with HUD homes for frosting and a big school as the middle decoration. The only store in the town is the tribe's smokeshop, which is a short cruise from my house where my Mom raised up my sister and I.

Annissa, my sister, and I come from different fathers. Her dad was an Indian guy from not too far from around where our Mom grew up. My father was from a small town called El Celitre in Jalisco, Mexico.

Our mom was a mixture of Paiute, Irish, and Mexican descent. She grew up on the reservation with the rest of our family, being raised by both my grandparents.

My father left when I was three, so our mom ended up working her ass off supporting us kids. She also took classes at the community college in her off-time which made it hard for her to be at home.

Between Mom's job and working toward her degree, my sister and I grew up doing the day care thing and spending a lot of time with our grandparents.

As I got into my early teens, I started hangin' down at the courts after school. "Hangin' with the kids" as some said. It was a funny thing; all these kids hanging out. What made it funny was that they were all related one way or another, so whoever came along just sort of rounded out the gene pool from their particular side of the family.

I hung out the most with my cousin George, or Sunch as he was better known. Both of us were the same age and in the same grade, so among all the other kids we had the most in common with each other.

We'd go down to the school in the evenings to watch the older kids play ball. We usually brought a ball to shoot around with on the side, but if we didn't there was always one laying around.

In those games the older guys played in, we used to watch and watch. Back then, every little thing was such a big deal. I remember watching those guys jump so high you could see the shit they wrote on the bottom of their shoes. A young kid would be dazzled by the way they rose up and floated sweet "jumpers" off their fingertips, through the air, straight to the bottom of the chain nets making a loud 'clang.'

Us kids sometimes just kicked back to watch and laugh as they talked smack to each other all up and down the court. Sometimes it came to blows, but for the most part it was peaceful. The only trouble that showed up came in the form of drunk fools that always showed up with something to say. They usually got knocked out, rolled off the court, and the game went on.

Sunch and I practiced our game everyday. We'd plan out how we'd burn those guys if we did th is to 'em, or if they tried this move on us. We even sharpened up at the largely under-appreciated art of smack-talking. For that, we'd sit in at home listening to old Eddie Murphy and 2 live crew tapes. We were preparing all the time for the day when we'd have to step in. As it turned out that wasn't exactly over night.

In their eyes, we were just kids. If we wanted to play we had to play on the little courts with the bent up, seven foot rims that everybody dunked on. That court sucked not just because of that, but the pavement had all kinds of missing pieces and the rims never had nets. The only time it ever got played on was by real little kids or when the bigger guys practiced their dunks.

Size was the only thing that keeping us on the sidelines. We were just too small. The bigger guys came in all shapes, sizes, and even color. You had fat guys that were light, skinny guys who were dark, and the real cool guys disappeared after sunset no matter what size they were.

Through all the different people, there were some that were the more memorable.

Big Ivan, he was a graduate from the "Charles Barkley School of Ball." Straight muscle to the hole was his game. On the court if he got the arm, later on he'd give the hammer. Also a recognized rebounding machine, he took no prisoners in the paint when it came to chalking up 'boards.'

On offense Big Ivan would drive the middle every chance he could, and no matter how hard a bash was or how brutal a hack got laid, his shot always got off. Granted, some weren't the prettiest shots ever, but at least they still got up there. The chances of those shots going in wasn't all that great either, but there's just something you respect about a player who could take a hit then never end up crying like a little bitch.

Another of the stars was Primeaux (pronounced 'Pree-moe'). Speed was what he brought to the game. His fast breaks and high endurance rose the game's tempo past the point of what would normally be just another hour long "cherry-picking" session, which tended to happen from time to time.

His shooting ability was average and his dribbling could've used polish, but the momentum created by him enveloped the whole court. Once the ball gets moving so fast up and down the court, it's impossible for anybody to just stand around. That ended up making some good games.

Aside from that, he also showed up with some funky haircuts, even for back then. Pony tails, shaved sides, a mohawk, little braids, little mohawk-braids, those were just some of the doo's Primeaux sported.

Primeaux's historical fame came when he went down in history as the first person in town to get the Reebok pumps when they first came out. Everybody stood around and stared at the almighty shoe that was to 'revolutionize the game.' When he first stepped on the court with them, I pestered like a fly until he let me press the air release button. Even today, I remember the loud "Ssss!" it made and how excited I got off it. I feel like a stupid ass looking back on it today, but in times like those, stupid shit like that made your day.

Brutality in the raw, fresh doo's, and pumps belonged to those guys but style came with only one man: Big Mike Wads. He was the only kid who went to school off the reservation and had anything to show for it. He played varsity football, basketball, and baseball for Reed High School up in Reno, and he was the one I looked up to the most. Always wearin' his game face, even in his sleep some said, not only could the man ball, but he had that ever-so-eloquent trait know as class.

What helped Big Mike a lot was that turning eighteen in our tribe meant big bucks, and Big Mike wasn't afraid to show it. A couple weeks after you turn eighteen, you get a check in the mail for twenty grand and some change. At this particular time, Big Mike was the "money man."

Everyday Big Mike rolled up to the front of the school with the top dropped in his brand new Capri bumpin' his system. He'd sit there bobbin' his head to the beats that bump sizin' up the competition for the day. Sometimes he sat there doing that for over ten minutes, while everybody was warming up, getting ready to play.

After that was done, he'd get out and pop his trunk that was full of the latest, most expensive Nikes and take another five minutes deciding which pair was the right one to play in. When the right shoe was found and his presence was known, Big Mike kicked his amp up and did the "Big Mike's walk" on down to the court to clock in.

Big Mike was one of the few guys that could actually dunk, which made him closer to being "The Man" than a lot of people.

Big Mike was just too cool, back then. Everything he did I wanted to do. He chewed, so I started dipping in Skoal and Copenhagen. Big Mike bought all the latest rap on the market, so every trip up to the mall picked up Big Mike's weekly top ten. Big Mike also had the habit of leaning back to scratch his nuts, so much to my mom's disgust, I scratched them too. Mine, not his.

All these guys skill level qualified them as badass players, but there was one that stood out above them all.

At the head of every court sits a king. That's universal, whether your talking about the ghetto, el barrio, the 'burbs, or in this case the rez. There's always someone who can make the court shake just by setting foot on it.

While some guys sported cool doo's, speed, or had soul coming out the assholes, some just come to play ball, and that's exactly what he did.

Weylen was his name and no one ever needed to ask his game. All you needed to do was sit back and watch as he punished nets and made even the thought of defending him a waste of time.

From the moment he came on the court he craved the ball like a tweeker craves a fat line, and once he got a hold of it, "forget about it." He only missed if he wanted to. If he want to make that pass straight through your defense and make you feel like a dumb shit he'd do that too.

He'd scored over sixty points during high school games, and there were countless other nights where, if we were keeping books, he would've been in triple digits. The guy's first step was so quick, he'd blow by you, make the score, then be back in front of you before you even noticed he was gone. His arsenal of moves and speed made up for his size, he wasn't even close to what's considered tall in today's game. His shot glided just over defending hands, almost making fun of someone for trying to stop it. Speaking from experience, I can tell you that was almost a mission impossible. Weylen played so good it made your dick hard.

Putting all these guys together put Pyramid Lake on the map as far as Indian tournaments go. We'd travel all over the west to watch those guys play against teams from all over.

Time passed and us little fools turned into big fools and finally got a chance to mix it up with those big dawgs. Sunch dropped bombs from long range and I muscled it out boards from inside the paint. We were still just "rookies" and the didn't get picked towards the end, but we still got to play.

In the category of skill, Sunch excelled a lot faster than I did. He put up decent numbers and moved up in when they chose teams. Every game I'd be down in the trenches catchin' elbows and gettin' big asses jabbed in my gut.

Seasons went by and ball was life, after school for us and work for those older guys. Everyday down at the courts putting in work, taking my hits, and talking smack, it seemed like it was never gonna end.

The strength and support some people find at church or in bars was sort of what we found on the court. Shitty days dropped through the net with the flick of the wrist, and for those couple hours nothing could touch us.

Through rain, sleet, and hangovers, game was on 'til sundown, sometimes even past that. Everyday with no exceptions, then on weekends we'd party, carry on, and snag out.

Mondays were business as usual. Everybody ended up back on the blacktop sportin' hickeys and laughing at who was stupid enough to get with their own cousin.

More time went by and people started showing up less. A few here and there, then hardly anybody came at all. Sunch and I stopped to look around and what we saw was the older guys settling down.

Homies that couldn't be seen without ball-in-hand now had to ask permission to even touch one. Bellies got bigger, cheeks got chubbier, and sneakers weren't so sneaky. Hardtop legends known as "Big Ivan" or "Big Mike" now took on the titles of "Daddy" or "Honey." Blacktop warriors once feared and respected now got laughed out when we'd see them pushing strollers up and down the street. Fellas that ran up and down the court with endless energy now sat at home watching "Happy Days" reruns and eating twinkies.

Court attendance took a nosedive until we were the only ones. Everybody had gone out and grown up. Having neither job or steady woman, Sunch and I were forced into hours of one-on-one and 21. On weekends, the only ones to pass our cheap booze to was each other. Even the snags disappeared, chicks who were always down to pound got knocked up or up and went respectable on us.

"It happens to the best of them," the man once wrote. Our mentors sold out to the world and became what young, single, free men fear. They were now what's known back home as "old bastards."

Old bastards are those guys you see at the store renting videos on Friday nights. You go up to ask them what's up and their woman answers for them. To go party they have to get on their knees and beg for permission or sneak out like some twelve year old kid.

To become an old bastard is to be condemned to a life of holding the purse, pushing the shopping carts with the fucked up wheel, and changing loaded diapers by the case.

Seeing our idols go and slop out like that really messed with us. It was hard trying not to laugh at one of your homies when you see him crying around in the middle of the supermarket over some chick who has him "whooped." It's stuff like that, that makes you want to just say, "fuck it," but we kept on.

The courts faded into history. The new generation of kids was more into gangbangin', tweekin' out, or just smokin' weed all the time. The older guys always had to be home by dark, so Sunch and I eventually did end up losing hope. This signaled the end of the "Golden Age" at the courts.

Hard times followed but like anything you learn to accept it. Giving up those times up was tough but I've grown to appreciate them and the people I shared them with. Without those courts I would've never learned how to make "a two-step juke" or even techniques on the use of the infamous "G-spot."

Maybe one day off in the future we'll get together again. We'll sit our big asses down together, grab the beer out the fridge, kick all the women out the house and just talk about those old times. While our kids are out shootin', talkin', and scratchin' themselves laughing around at us old bastards.

EPILOGUE

Sunch-Now referred to as the infamous "Munch Man," he lives back home in Wads. He received his GED and is now an apprentice in ironworking. Doesn't play much ball, Sunch/Munch Man takes it easy these days at home with his daughter.

Allen Primeaux-Still living on the rez, Primeaux became a smoke jumper for a fire crew in Nevada. He's presently a tribal cop for the tribe. Has been known to show up down at the old gym, now and then. Currently sports the regulation crew cut.

Weylen Johns-After leading the mighty Pyramid Lake Lakers to two state titles, Weylen went on to become a father. He's now raising his kids back in Wads with his woman. Frequents the old gym with his brother-in-law, the uncanny "Jiz."

Big Ivan-After settling down and having a little girl, Ivan retired from the game and, after an unfortunate incident, is now serving 80 years in federal prison, along with his sister Paula, for two counts of second-degree murder and illegal discharge of a firearm on federal land.

Big Mike Wads-Nobody really knows what happened to Big Mike. Rumors had it that he's living in Reno with his woman. It's also said that he had a kid too, but no one really knows for sure. If anyone sees a kid walking around bobbin' his head and itchin' himself, they'll know who to blame.

Gabe(the Narrator)-Well, Gabe eventually moved off the rez and graduated from high school in Carson City. He's waiting to receive his associate's degree in Creative Writing at the Institute of American Indian Arts. After that, his plans include film studies in Canada with the hope that one day he'll make a movie about all these crazy fools and the ones too rugged to mention in here.

127

NONFICTION

SAYING GOODBYE

Dawn Lazore was once my friend. Kawi is passed and gone now like yesterday's storm. Her friends called her Kawi, short for her Indian name, Kawisiiosta. She was eighteen when she was brutally beaten to death, just a couple of weeks shy of her nineteenth birthday.

Kawi's loss was devastating to everyone who knew her. Kawi was the first person I ever lost who was close to me. I had known Kawi for seven years and in those seven years we had become very close. When I was told that she was gone, my mind ran 90 miles an hour with flashes of memories we had together. The pain of loss split through me like I had swallowed a razor, sharpened to perfection. My heart was broken. My eyes swelled with hot tears, as I fell to the blue carpeted floor, numb from shock. Days, months passed me by without a will to do anything but swim in my sorrows for my lost friend. To me, it seemed nothing mattered anymore. It took me a long time to get over the death of my friend, Kawi.

Kawi was a beautiful person and her strong native features separated her from my other friends. Her hair was black with a slight tint of blue. Her eyes were also black like a raven's feathers. When Kawi smiled, she showed off her straight, even teeth of glittering whiteness. Kawi's beauty made her strong and confident.

The memories linger in my mind. They don't hurt as much anymore. My memories of us, Kawi and I, actually make me smile and glad because that is all I have left of our once lively friendship. The memory that pops into mind right this minute is the time Kawi and I played quarter shots. Usually you play quarter shots with alcohol but we didn't have any. So, we used whatever was in the fridge: milk, kool-aid, juice, soda, water, and even coffee. We filled an eight-ounce glass and tried to get a quarter into the shot glass by bouncing the quarter off the table top.

Kawi was the one to get her quarter in first, every time. Unfortunately that made me the loser and I had to drink up what was in the glass. After the tenth glass or so I wasn't feeling so great. I felt like a balloon with just a tad too much air and there was a needle near by for some action. I booked it outside and sure enough the needle popped my balloon and I began throwing up the multicolored liquid that had inflated my stomach.

I was crouched over in misery, tears running down my cheeks and snot gurgling out of my nose, while Kawi was jumping up and down, clapping her hands like an excited child at her first circus, shrieking, "A waterfall, a waterfall!" After I was done, we sat out on the porch laughing at what seemed a never ending laugh. That was just one of our many memories together.

I think it was the moment I was told of Kawi's death that all the bad times we shared disappeared, vanished like a magician's hat trick. They're still there but they're hidden, unseen, unheard. To me, just the good memories remained. One moment in particular stayed fresh in my mind after Kawi died. The week before she died, we both were invited to this party. While I was at the party I only saw her once. She was across the room and we glanced at each other, just a glance, like seeing a falling star. You don't dare turn your head for you'd miss it. "If I only knew that was going to be the last time I'd seen her alive?" That thought still runs through my mind now and then but I know I will never get an answer.

Kawi-Dawn always had something to say. There was never silence when she was around. Kawi was the kind of person who kept the party going, going for hours, even days and she was the only person who could make me laugh just hearing her laugh. It's hard to recall what she sounded like but I can imagine her now and I smile. Kawi was outspoken. She was the kind of person to say what she felt about anything or anyone. She made a lot of enemies that way but she didn't give a shit what anyone thought of her. I envied that she didn't give a shit what people thought.

At the funeral Kawi had an open casket. Kawi was beaten so severely nobody recognized her. It made me mad that she had an open casket. Kawi didn't even look human. What I saw was and wasn't the person I once knew. When I saw her I tried to hold back my tears, I can still feel the lump that consumed my throat and the pain in my heart. I felt like running out of the longhouse. I felt like running forever and ever. Once I was outside, my family came over, secured me with their loving arms. At that point I released everything I had building up inside, out.

Kawi Lazore was my best friend. Kawi was young and she was beautiful. She could have been anything. Kawi had her whole life ahead of her. The one thing she wanted to do most was travel. She was denied her dreams. As I fulfill my dreams, I will always have Kawi with me in mind, heart and in spirit.

Dawn "Kawi" Lazore is passed and gone now like yesterday's rain storm. The damage from the storm remains and my memories are not forgotten. Everyone knows not long after every rain storm there comes a rainbow. My rainbow did not come right away but when it did, it brought hope and new growth began as the sunlight shined on my saddened face. With the sunlight came a smile and I became stronger, taller and happier once again.

It's been over four years now since Kawi's been gone. Over the four years there has been only one feeling I cannot seem to shake and probably never will: Kawi, I miss you!

A TRIP INTO REALIZATION

On January 14, 1993, I had just left a party and was driving down St. Regis Road towards "the point." "The point" was a parking lot across from the St. Regis church where my so-called friends, drunks, crack/dope heads, acid freaks and just plain stupid kids with nothing to do, would go. We would fill up the parking lot on Friday and Saturday nights to "hang out" while some of those same so-called friends' grandparents, aunts and other family members would gather in the same parking lot on Sunday mornings. Their cars' tires would be the victims of broken glass. Their eyes would show their disgust and sadness for the younger generations as they walked in their best clothes through the parking lot towards the church. Funny thing happened that night. I pulled into the parking lot, there was not a single person there. I sat in my 1988, Cutlass Oldsmobile with the radio playing *Sign* by Ace of Base. I waited for a couple minutes but not one car went by. Finally, I reached in my right pants pocket and pulled out a foil wrapper that I had stashed for the right time. It had just began snowing outside when I popped four hits of blotter acid. I was determined to have a good time no matter what, so I put my car into drive, turned the wheel as far left as I could and stomped on the accelerator. My head jerked back as my "ol' girl" began whipping her rear end around and around. I kept my eye on the church as a focus point while I went flying in a dizzy spell. Suddenly, I could hear bottles clanging in my back seat. I immediately stopped to investigate. My thumb flicked the button for the interior light as I looked into the back seat. There on the floor behind the passenger seat was a case of Budweiser beer with only a few bottles missing. Earlier that night I had lent out my car to one of my friends' cousins, Leonard. "He must've forgot it when he went back to the party," I thought to myself. I had planned to go back to the party, but the acid I had just taken was kicking in and there was no way I was going back there.

The snowflakes were falling even thicker as I drove back up St. Regis Road. I was the only vehicle out and the roads were getting covered with snow. Then for some reason I didn't feel right. I looked over to the passenger side and my window was fucked up. It was fucking fucked up, busted. I freaked. Just then someone in a truck was flashing their lights at me, but I didn't stop because I knew who it was. It was a guy that I met at the party and Leonard, the guy who I trusted with my car. By this time the acid was playing with my vision and my mind. I drove right past the party, right past my house. I knew if I went home Leonard would go there and my mother was home. I couldn't have that because I would get into trouble. I couldn't go home so I decided to go to my brother and his family's apartment. They lived about twenty miles away. During this time the snow was falling even harder then before and I was seeing the world through stoned eyes.

The straight road that I was driving on was curving and the swaying trees alongside the road were outlined in red, blue, purple, and yellow. My vision was messing me up and I was driving on the shoulder just a few inches from the ditch. I was concentrating so hard that I had to turn the radio off and my face was an inch away from the windshield. "Please, don't go in the ditch, I can make it. It's only another mile," were the words that kept passing through my mind. Finally, I pulled into the parking lot of the Massena Village Apartments. A sense of relief overwhelmed me as I found an empty parking space. I turned the key and took it out of the ignition as I sat back to relax and breathe. I searched my jacket pocket for a cigarette and found a joint I had bought before I went to the party. I wanted to save it so I stepped out of the car into the cold winter air. Snow flakes melted as they landed on my face. The parking lot lights were hurting my eyes as I looked up to see if my brother's lights were on. I walked fast trying to avoid anyone that might be looking out their windows. As I started up the stairs to the second story, I began remembering my busted window and the truck, and wished I knew what had happened. I reached the door and for some reason I wanted to run back down the stairs, out the door and for some reason I wanted to run back down the stairs, out the door, jump into my car, and take off. But I knew one thing for sure, I didn't want to drive through that fucking blizzard again. I was stuck. I knocked on the door and leaned against the wall, waiting for an answer. A minute passed, and there was no answer, so I took my license out of my back pocket and used it to open the door. After several tries I managed to get the door open, and slowly walked in. "Hello, is there anyone home?" I said aloud. To hear my own voice was startling and it seemed to echo through the empty apartment. After realizing no one was home, I sat on the couch searching for my cigarettes and lighter. I took a cigarette from the pack and placed it in my mouth, still looking for a lighter. With no luck I began searching the couch, cupboards, and dressers for a lighter or matches. About a half an hour later I still had no luck. Even the stove wasn't working.

An hour went by since I had walked into the apartment and the acid I took was still working its tricks on me. I knew that I would be tripping for another eight hours at the most. I wouldn't sleep, smoke, or leave until the acid wore off. I began wondering where my family went. Their groceries were still in paper bags on the floor by the door. It was as if they got home from shopping and vanished with no trace.

By now the ceiling had flowery patterns slowly moving counter clockwise. My head was tingling; my stomach had a hollow feeling to it and I needed a cigarette or joint badly. At some point I wanted to get that case of Bud out of the back seat of my car, but I was too paranoid someone was going to see me. So, I laid there on the couch watching the tricks that the acid played on me. The rug was full of different colors waving to the rhythm of my heartbeat. The walls were twisting and untwisting as I lay watching, enjoying the feeling of being stoned to the point of no return. Just then I remembered my windshield again, but I knew it was no use worrying about it until I talked to Leonard.

For some reason my brother's voice popped into my head, "I don't want you to take acid, but you can take mushrooms. Mushrooms are natural." Then my mother's voice popped into my head saying, "I would rather you smoke weed than drink alcohol." Finally my oldest brother's voice popped into my head, "Guy (my nickname), I don't care if you drink but you better not do coke or I will beat the shit out of you. You know I love you." Up to that point my trip was going fine, but now I wanted to be normal and I couldn't. For the next four hours I sat on my oldest brother's couch watching the sun come up, and looking at the pictures on the wall of my family staring back at me. Up to that moment in my life, I had been doing all the drugs that I could get my greedy little hands on for my own false pleasures. I never thought of my family when I was drinking, smoking that good skunk weed, and lining coke on the mirror that I kept in the trunk of my car for emergencies.

That morning of January 15, 1993 I came to realize the harm I was putting myself through, and the worry that my mother was feeling at nights when I wouldn't get home. I was an inconsiderate junkie that didn't appreciate anyone or anything, except artificial pleasures that drugs gave to me. Today, I wonder if I never took those four hits of acid would I still be hurting the people that mean so much to me.

AMONG GIANTS

> It is not necessary to accept everything as true, one must only accept it as necessary.
> -Franz Kafka, *The Trial*

This is a true story:

Fact and fiction must coexist. Because with every true story there is a lie. No matter how much you think your story is true, there is someone who will tell you a different version of their side of the story. And their story is also true.

With all fiction there is always a bit of truth. I can't tell you that what you are about to read is a true story because memory isn't a kind beast.

You see, the problem with memory is that it tends to play tricks on you. It makes you remember things that may not have happened, or remember things in a different order than you thought. Remembering things can be dangerous and even painful .

Though my memory isn't as good as it should be, I'm going to present the facts to you as best as I can remember–only the truth.

I can't remember if my father was an abusive person. But I can remember late nights when he and my mother would be fighting, and I would be in my room crying. I remember that once he tore the screen door off of its hinges. I had witnessed it and became afraid of my father.

My father was a big man. Even now he is, but not in the way that I envisioned him as a kid. When I was a child, he was very big. I always imagined him as a giant. But then again, when I was that young, everyone was a giant.

Ever since I can remember I always wanted to be a writer. My mother used to always tell people that before I could even write I was always reciting stories to her or telling her poems that I made up. Then she started writing them down for me. That was when she taught me to read and write. By the time I turned three, I was writing my own stories and reading as many books as I could find around the house. After I finished all of the books in the house–I was about four and a half–my brother started walking with me to the library almost every day, and I proceeded to read every book there. I cherished my library card.

I didn't finish going through all of the books at the library. I stopped somewhere around C. I realized that a lot of the books I was reading were dross. It was then that I started being selective about the books I read. I would pick a favorite author or I would read a story based on the plot synopsis on the book jacket.

When I was about five, my aunt bought for me _The Count of Monte Cristo_. It became my favorite book. I would carry it with me and read it and reread it until the pages came loose and fell out. I liked the story about the revenge and how this man spent many years preparing for that revenge and making his escape.

There were a lot of things back then that I'd like to remember and have forgotten. Then there are things that I wished I never remembered. But, as I said, memory is a strange beast.

My mother died in May, and I was cleaning out things from her house when I happened to run across a lot of my childhood things. A broken yo-yo that I would never throw away. My slingshot that I started to make but never finished. Then I found a box that was full of papers. On those papers were a lot of the stories and poems that I wrote as a kid. I read through the stories and laughed at what a terrible writer I was, and I also found these little drawings that I did. There was a comic book that I drew, _Super Guy_, was the name of it. It was a parody of Superman. It never got finished. And the drawing was worse than the writing.

I laughed as I looked through these things and hoped that no one but me saw these terrible stories. Then as I continued searching through the box, I came across a journal that I had started writing when I was four.

The pages were loose and some were missing, but I read through them, and a lot of what was written I didn't understand. Then, there were some things in there that I didn't understand then but understand now. I don't remember much about the past. There were happy memories and there were some sad. But what I do remember is that my world was ruled by giants...

November 1, 1977

Faith is in the hospittle again. Last time she had to go to the hospittle was when she fell down the stairs and broke her hand. Then 1 time Dady pulled her by the arm because she wouldn't come to him when he called her and it pulled her arm out of a sockit or something like that. I don't know why she was in the hospitlle now. They sad something about how she got stabbed with a close hanger and I guess it cut her up inside. We went to see her yessterday before we went out trick or treeting. She was crying. My Dady came in and she cried more. Momy told him to leave.

Dady took us trick or treeting. He was a wolf. Before we went out he scared me and my brother. he was hiding in bushes and jumped out. My Dady is sometimes scary. He gets mad and loses his temper. Momy says its becuss of work. He has a hard day.

We walked with Dady and my frends were scared of him

Me and Chris wanted to go to Mr Daviss house but Dady wouldnt let us. He said Mr Davis put sinide in the candy to hurt little kids. I dont know what sinide is but its probably good becuss I always liked Mr Daviss place. He had the best candy. Momy used to take us there all the time.

I dug further through the box and came across some drawings. One was a drawing of my family. There was my brother, Chris, skinny and pale. Then there was my sister, Faith, lying in the bed, and my mother holding my hand. Beside me was my father. I drew him tall and strong. Under that drawing I found another loose paper which was an entry to my journal.

July 6, 1976
Last nite Chris didnt go to sleep til late. I was already asleep when he did. He woke me in the middle of the nite. He was crying. I didn't say anything to him I was scared Dady yelled from there room, shut up boy or Ill give you more. Ill give you a real reason to cry. Then my brother cried not so loued. this morning I got up and saw blood stains in the middle of the bed where he was laying. I walk into the kitchen and he told Momy that it hurt when he sat down. He sad he used the bathroom and there was blood. He wanted to go to the doctor. Momy was washing dishes and crying. She told him, no everythings going to be all rite. She said it wont hurt long.

Later this afternoon my Brother was taking off his under wer and there was blood on the back of it. I ask him what happened. He sad he fell on the road and cut hisself inside. I remember during Christmas me and my Cousin were putting decerashins on a Christmas tree. We fell down, I fell on one of those tree decorashins shaped like a house with a point sticking up and it cut my booty. If I didnt hold out my hand before I fell it would have probably stabbed me inside my booty hole. Maybe the same thing kinda happened to him.

What happened with the tree decoration thing was that, late one night, my cousins and I found a camera at Pokni's and Papa's house (my grandparents). We all gathered around the Christmas tree. We were going to pretend like we were going to be hanging ornaments like they do in family photos. There were about seven of us around the tree posing. Me, Tony, and Warren were standing on a small chair doing our pose. When the camera flashed, Tony lost his balance, knocking me and Warren over. Now let me explain to you, Warren was really fat back then and so when we both toppled over like a pair of dominoes, we landed on top of the television. I held my hand out to break my fall. And as we fell onto the television, I felt this ornament of a church's steeple scratching my left butt cheek. But I couldn't move or get up because Warren was on top of me, and I was using all of the strength that I could to keep this ornament from entering my orifice. I kept yelling for him to get off of me. Eventually, after many minutes, he did–keeping me from hurting inside.

December 12, 1980
2 days ago Chris got shot. Me and mom came home and he was bleeding on the couch. He sad he was messing with the 22 in the closet and it went off and shot him. Me and my mom were crying on the way to the hospital. It was scary. Chris was lying in the back seat with towels wrapped around his gun shot wound. We got to the hospital. I seen my principle he...

It ends there. The paper was ripped and I can't find the other half. See, this is where memory plays tricks on me. The way I remembered it is that I saw a little bit of blood in the yard and there were a couple of drips on the porch. I ran inside wondering what happened because I knew my brother was suppose to be there. Then that was when we found him on the couch. But what I wrote in my journal says something different. So maybe it's good to keep an account of things that go on. So you can get the facts straight.

January 25, 1978

   Mommy finally came home. She said she went to visit Aunt Pearl. Daddy went to pick her up in the middle of the night. I guess daddy didn't know she was coming home and made us get out of bed and drove around. I guess he didnt know where to find mommy. He was cussing again. He stopped the car at the gas station. I told him I wanted a pop. He told me to shut up. He was on the phone getting angry. He then drove to Mr. Davis's house. Mr Davis must of picked her up.

   When we got there he told us to stay in the car and we were cold. I didn't wear a jacket and he didn't have the warmer on. He got mommy and took her into the car. She was crying and hugged Chris in the front seat. She must have missed us and been sad. She must have been tired to. She looked like she had been sleeping. Though it was cold she was sweating.Daddy was outside yelling at Mr. Davis. Mr. Davis was wearing a robe. Daddy was yelling at him. I couldn't understand him becaus the windows were rowed up. Then daddy started hitting Mr. Davis. It was kind of funny because Mr Davis's robe came open and he didnt have no underwear on and we could see his booty. when we left Mr. Davis was still laying on the ground.

Not long after that, Jon Davis got married. He married my teacher, Miss Williams. It was weird trying to adjust to her name change. Over Christmas break, they got married and she came back saying she is now Mrs. Davis. Every once in a while, I would slip up and call her Miss Williams. I was happy for her that she married Jon Davis. When I was a kid, I secretly wanted Jon to be my father.

He was always nice to me. He worked at the drug store where my mom always took us to buy ice cream. He was always patting my head and telling my mother how much I had grown. While he worked behind the counter, he would look up at the same time as I did, and smile and wink at me. He would always put extra ice cream in my sundae with an extra cherry.

I thought that my mother and Jon were once in love with each other. Maybe they were once high school sweethearts or something. Sometimes I worry that she had an affair with him. That's what the above sounds like now that I've read it over and thought about it. But these are ideas and theories – not facts.

The fact was that my mother took us to the drug store almost every day. We would sit in a booth and eat ice cream. When my mother was in the drugstore, she would become a totally different person. Around the house, she hardly smiled, and was usually sad. My father's arguing with her probably brought a lot of stress on her.

But when my mother was in the drugstore, she was a beautiful person. She would talk to Jon and they would laugh together. It was great to see her smile. Once, Jon told her a joke and she laughed so hard, her coke float came out of her nose, and she laughed loudly again. Then she told Jon a joke and they laughed together. I never thought my mother knew any jokes. Now I realize how much of a mystery my mother was.

Then after my father and Jon got into that argument, we almost never went to the drugstore.

When I entered high school, the drugstore became a favorite hang out for me and my friends. Jon would give me a free root beer float, ask me how I was doing in school, and he always asked about my mother.

I just noticed that now I call Mr. Davis, Jon. What happened was, when I was very young, I guess around seven or eight, I was waiting for my mother in the drug store while she was at Bruton's buying some clothes for my sister. He had me sit at the counter while he made me a sundae. When he handed me the sundae, he also gave me a ten dollar bill and said, "Here, this is yours. You keep it."

Now, when you're nine years old, ten dollars is a lot of money. You think that it's probably around a million. So I was really happy. I smiled and said, "Thank you, Mr. Davis."

He smiled and said, "Please don't call me Mr. Davis. Call me..." he paused briefly, but it was enough for me to notice. Then he said, "It's Jon – call me Jon." When I was a kid, I continued calling him Mr. Davis because my mother told me that some people think that it isn't polite to call them by their first name. But when I got into high school, and spent my time at the drugstore, I started calling him Jon.

It's funny how I always wondered what it would be like to have Jon Davis as my father, because he was probably a better father than my biological father. While I was a teenager, and started hanging out at the drug store, I would talk to him and tell him many things – some of them were things I couldn't share with anyone else. We became very close. He became like a best friend to me. Once, I told him how I wanted to be a writer. He got all excited and told me that was great. After that, I told him the plots to many of my stories. He told me to write them down before I forget them. He was the first person to ever read any of my work.

Then one day, I told him about how I was in love with Shannon Smith. Shannon was the most beautiful girl in school. I had known her since eighth grade, and probably had a crush on her for just as long.

Once, I brought her in the drug store with me. She sat at the booth while I went up to the counter to get us a couple of floats. He asked me if she was Shannon and I said, yeah. He went over and talked to her, asked who her parents and grandparents were. He asked her all sorts of questions, and bragged on me, stuff like that. I'm sure that if it were my mother or father that did this, I'd probably be dead embarrassed or something. But I didn't mind him asking her these questions.

Later that week, I came in by myself, and he asked me if I was dating her now. I told him, "No, we're still friends. I don't know if she likes me."

He then said, "Well, you won't know until you ask. You've got a fifty-fifty chance. Anyway, what's the worst she gonna do? She'll just say no. She's your friend so she won't spit on you or anything, and after she says no, she might change her mind. And if you ask her, and she says no, you'll still be in the same place as you were when you asked her. Then if she says yes, you'll be in a better place than before."

"I don't know," I said. "I doubt she wants a zit-faced kid."

I never did ask her out. I got sick and missed school for a couple of days. When I returned, I found her holding hands with Pancho O'Dell. I would like to say that if I didn't see the two of them holding hands, I would have asked her out. But, truthfully, I doubt that I would have.

After that I started going out with Priscilla Parsons. I didn't care for her, but she was the only girl that would go out with me. She fell in love with me. When she told me that she loved me, I started to avoid her.

Then we were both at a party, and Priscilla kept trying to talk to me. I ignored her. Then she found me talking to Gretchen Hostler, and I had my arm around her. Priscilla started yelling at me then. I *told her to leave me alone, and I walked away with Gretchen.*

Fifteen minutes later, they found Priscilla in the bathroom. She had slit her wrist with a busted beer bottle.

The ambulance came and I rode with them to the hospital. Priscilla slept that night and I left.

I didn't return until two days later. She was awake and started yelling at me as soon as I walked in the room. I calmed her down. She told me that she did everything for me. She continually repeated that she loved me. I told her not to waste her time. Then she slapped me with her unbandaged hand.

I then told her that what she did was stupid and not to ever do anything like that again – especially for a guy. She then told me not to talk to her again. I never did.

I wish I could say that I was nice to her, but I don't remember doing or saying anything nice. Now I wish I could have told her that I did care about her and wished her happiness, and all that. But I never did. After that, I'd see her around, but I never said anything to her, even though, sometimes, I wanted to ask how she was doing.

I heard that after high school, she married a doctor and moved to Dallas.

Most of my friends blamed me for her attempted suicide and said that I was a bastard for the way I acted towards her. Shannon wasn't extremely upset but said that I handled that situation wrong. She said I should have told her that I didn't love her the first time, instead of ignoring her like I did.

I learned my lesson, and now I try to be truthful with a woman, and not be so rude towards them. But I do still find myself being shy around women. I sometimes think that they wouldn't have an acne-scarred young man.

June 21, 1979
I turn 9 years old today. It was fun. I got a lot of neat toys. Tony bought me a car model. I had my birthday party at the lake. I swam alot and got proon fingers. When we got home mom gave me a present and said its from Mr. Davis. I opened it up. It was Spiderman Crime Lab. It was cool. I like Mr. Davis. I wish he came to the party. But I think him and dad don't like each other. *That was weird to read. I can't believe I liked a birthday party. I don't like having parties now. I don't even like to acknowledge my birthday.*

Birthday parties are usually depressing and full of people that you don't really know and don't care to know. Then, the people that show up that you have any remote interest in are friends that you see every day, anyway.

July 28, 1980

Today, me and my brother went walking into the woods. I found a turtle. I wanted to keep it. My brother told me to leave it alone. He said the turtle don't want to be bothered.

Last night I was laying on the couch watching TV. Dad said I should just wear my underwear because its cooler. I did. He was in his underwear too and came and layed on the couch with me. Dad said he loved me. He put his arm around me and then mom walked in. She was mad. She sent me to the room again. I tried to listen but couldn't hardly hear them. They were arguing again.

Tomorrow we're suppose to go to the movies with my uncle. I can't wait.

Okay, I kind of remember what happened here. I don't remember where my brother and sister were that night I was watching television. It was just me and my father, home alone, when my mother walked in. That night was the only time that I can remember him saying that he loved me, and the only time he hugged me. We hardly ever spent time with each other. He was either spending time with my sister or brother. He was usually in my sister's room or off somewhere with my brother. So, that night I felt really close to him.

Then my mother came home. She was mad at my father, so she sent me to the room. I went to my room but stood near the door and tried to listen. Then I opened the door and went to the kitchen. If they found me, I would lie to them and tell them I was getting some water. I listened to them and I can remember parts of the conversation but I only caught the middle of it and didn't exactly understand what they were arguing about. I always thought that my father was sleeping around with other women and my mother had just found out.

When I got close enough so that I could understand them, my mother was saying, "What about what you did to her? You knew she was pregnant, you bastard, and you made her kill the baby. She could've died, too."

"I was just thinking about her. I didn't want anyone to give her trouble, being so young with a baby."

"From now on, I don't want you to touch her. I don't want you to touch any of them."

"Don't tell me what I can or can't do."

Then I got braver and walked to the kitchen door, and cracked open the door to watch my parents. My mother said, "I swear to God, if you ever touch any of them again, I'll, I'll..." She looked at him and she was shaking. Then she said, "I don't know what I'll do, and you don't want to know what I'll do, but you just stay away from them."

He said, "I've heard it all before." Then he grabbed her and started kissing her. I didn't want to watch that so I went to my room. I guess they made up because they were sleeping together the next morning.

December 28, 1980

Christmas was fun. I got all kinds of toys. Me and Chris got these air guns and I like it. We knew we was going to get them before Christmas. We always know what we're gonna get before we get them. They always tried to keep them hidden. Most of the time it's in the closet in their room. Sometimes it's outside in the outside closet. Sometimes we don't always find all of them, but if we look good enough there somewhere around here.

Mom had a black eye. She said that someone opened a door when she was by it and it hit her. Then she said I shouldn't be so nosy.

I wish I was a grown up. When your a kid you never here what the grown ups say. They're always quiet whenever I'm around. As soon as I walk into the room they be quiet. But Christmas Eve night, I snuck by the door and listened to them talk. Mom and Papa was talking. He was telling her that everything's going to be all right. She was crying. He said that everything will be taken care of and that it'll probably look like an accident. She said she was scared. He gave her a hug. They was quiet for a while and so I walked in. Uncle T was in there to. He saw me and came up to me and I asked what was the matter with mom. He said that she was upset because some of the stuff she was cooking got burned. He took me into the living room where everyone was. Why do adults always lie?

Not long after that I quit writing my journal. I guess a part of it was that I was growing up and my brother was always teasing me, telling me that little girls write diaries. But, I think that what really got me to stop writing was what happened four days after New Years, 1981. I can remember clearly what happened that day, no matter how hard I try to keep it out of my mind.

The night before, me and my brother told our parents that we were going to walk to the park after school to play basketball. They said that it was all right. My mother then told my sister that she should go to Pokni's house. She said that she's going to come home late and she didn't want her be home alone. My sister said okay.

Then that next day, when we arrived at school, Chris forgot the basketball. So after school, we rode the bus back home, and after we'd get the basketball, we'd walk back to the park. We went into the house and couldn't find the basketball. Then my brother said that it's probably out in the garage. We went out there to look for it, and as we walked past the car, which we thought wasn't going to be there, we found our father sitting in the front seat, and it looked like he was sleeping. He had left the car running, and so we tried to wake him up to tell him that the he had left it on. He remained sleeping. We tried to open the doors but they were all locked.

My brother started hitting on the window with his fist to try and wake my father up. He remained still. His eyes were still open and it looked like he was looking directly at me. My brother was getting panicky. He was breathing hard and looked around to find a way to get into the car.

At first, I didn't fully comprehend what was going on. I thought that my father was only sleeping. Then when I saw my brother starting to panic, I knew that there was something wrong, and I started to get scared too.

My brother found a cinder block and threw it through the back window. He opened the door and crawled to the front seat. He reached over and turned off the car. He tried to shake my father awake, but he wouldn't wake. He told me to go call the ambulance. I ran into the house, and due to my panic, I dialed the number wrong the first time, and had to dial it twice.

I cried while my brother had his arm around me as we rode with our father in the back of the ambulance to the hospital. I remember how worried I was that they wouldn't find my mother or my sister, *and they wouldn't ever know what happened.*

My mother arrived an hour later. She never cried, but me and my brother did. My sister never came.

As the years passed, I never talked about what happened with my father and how I saw him in the car, with his mouth agape and his eyes half-opened, leaning against the driver side window, as if he was looking out at me. Staring at me.

I tried blocking that event out of my mind, but instead, I lost a lot of my other memories as I got older. But the memory of my father's suicide attempt always remained.

My mother and Jon became close friends again after that. Sometimes he and his wife would come over and visit or my mother would go over to his house to visit him.

Then, a year after that, I was at summer camp, and one day I noticed that the people there were acting strange. I knew something was wrong, because everyone was looking at me weird. Everyone was being nice to me. Then Kevin Bailey told me that I had to go home because of an emergency. So I packed up my bags and he drove me home in his van. We were mostly quiet on the whole trip.

When I arrived, my mother came out of the house. She held me and cried. I didn't know what was going on, and I got scared and confused. She let me go and wiped her tears away. She then told me that my sister had killed herself.

When I turned thirteen, my brother graduated from high school, and I didn't see him much after that. Then, two years ago, my brother ended up having a mental breakdown. He went to live with my mother until she died. Now he lives in the low rent housing projects. He pays two dollars on rent. Me and the rest of the family help support him and buy him food. I go to visit him every chance I get.

The other day, I went to visit him. He was eating a ham sandwhich while watching a small black and white T.V. that got bad reception. He was watching a documentary on wolves. He smelled as if he hadn't bathed for weeks, which is normal for him. When he smiled, you could see his gray teeth. I sat down and talked to him. He was wearing a pair of jeans and a brown work shirt.

I asked how he was doing. He said that his neighbors are trying to kill him. He said that he saw two black kids (except, he didn't use the word black kids) standing outside his apartment. He said that he knew that they were trying to rob his house, because that's what them people do.

He pointed out the window and showed me this old lady who was sitting outside on a bench. He said that woman has a gun in her house and she points it at him every time he goes outside. She's waiting for the right moment to shoot him. Besides being paranoid, he seems to be getting better.

Cindy, my recent girlfriend, had just left me. It was a week after my mother's funeral. We returned home from eating and that was when she told me that she was leaving. She said that she would have left me sooner, but only stayed because of my mother's funeral and she wanted to be supportive of me. She thought that maybe it was useless staying, because I displayed no emotion when I heard that she died. She said that at the funeral I acted the same, laughing around, making jokes. She was offended when I said, "My family's just dropping like flies, aren't they? First, my father, then my sister, then my brother, and now my mother. When's my time come?"

She also said that it was hard to put up with my mood swings. She said that one day I would be real happy and laughing and joking around. Then the next day, I would be all distant and quiet, and getting easily agitated. She didn't like how I always argued, even about some of the simplest things. Sometimes, I'd argue to her about a T.V. show she wants to watch, and I'd tell her the show wasn't any good as I turned the channel. Or I'd talk throughout the show as she tries to watch it, telling her all the reasons why the show isn't any good. Some nights we would argue, and I would do or say cruel things towards her and make her cry. I would then leave and not see or talk to her for days.

Before she left, she said, "In the three years that we've been together, you never once said you loved me. Maybe if you would've said or showed that you loved me I'd stay. But I feel nothing from you. You know, I have every right to hate you, but I can't. Even after all I've been through with you, I still love you. I hope that you'll be able to show your feelings to someone, otherwise you're gonna be lonely for the rest of your life."

Then she left, and I watched her through the window as she walked away. I could have stopped her and begged her to stay, but, truthfully, in all of the years we were together, I never loved her.

Jon attended my mother's funeral. He looked as if he hadn't slept—he had bags and circles under his eyes. His eyes were red. When he saw me, he came over to me and gave me a hug. He started crying and said that he was sorry and held me tight. I didn't know what to do so I gave him a hug back. He wouldn't let go. He continually said he was sorry. I didn't know what to say. I told him it was okay and patted him on the back. I finally got loose from his hold.

When he let go, he stood in front of me and didn't say anything for a long time. He just had his mouth open as if he was wanting to say something but didn't know how. Then he finally said, "Your mother was a good woman." Then he gave me another hug, but this one was not as long, and left.

After the funeral, I went to visit my father, who is now at a retirement home. He survived his attempted suicide but it put him in a coma. After he came out of the coma, he suffered severe brain damage. He's not aware of anything. He usually just sits in a wheel chair and stares out the window at one of the gardens. He doesn't even know who I am.

Every time I visit him, I pretend that he's still okay, and that he understands what I'm saying to him. That's what the doctor told me to do. I told him that my mother had a heart attack and died. Then I talked to him, I told him what all has been going on, and I told him the latest gossip. I sat with him and read the newspaper to him. He stared at the garden through his glassy eyes and spit dribbled down his chin. I took a wash cloth that was laying on his arm and wiped it away. I talked to him some more and then told him good-bye.

I went to see Jon at the drugstore. He gave me a free sundae. I sat at the counter while we talked. He had changed since my mother's death. It isn't an obvious change. It's just the way that he talks and the way that he moves. He slouches a lot more and doesn't smile as often as he used to.

He asked me that since I graduated from Haskell Indian Nations University, would I continue my education. I said that I didn't know. I told him how my mother wanted me to go to the Institute of American Indian Arts and study writing since I used to be such a good writer. I told my mother that I hadn't written anything in years. I then told Jon that I would like to go but it was probably too late to make it into class this fall, and I didn't think I could afford it.

He then told me that if I wanted to, and needed the money, he would help me out. I told him that I didn't know. It would be a while before I pay him back. He then told me that he owed it to me and my mother. He said that he would pay for my education, but only if I dedicated my first novel to him. He said that he remembered a lot of the stories that I let him read and the plot ideas that I would recite to him.

I thought about it for a few days. Then I sent a late registration in with a collection of stories that I had from my youth and about three stories that I had written within a week on Jon's computer.

After my final story was printed up, I put the stories in the envelope. He came in, handing me a glass of soda. He asked how it was going. I told him that I got finished and It's ready to be sent off.

After I sealed the envelope, I held the envelope in my hand, looked at it and said, "This is weird. I'm full of mixed feelings. I'm excited in that something good may come out of this, but I also have fear. What if they won't except me? What if I'm not as good a writer as I think I am? What if this doesn't work out and I end up wasting your money? What if I fail and end up stuck here in Broken Bow, working at Love's for the rest of my life?"

"Don't worry," he said. "Just remember this, it's okay to be afraid. Just as long as you have that hope."

I just smile at him. I don't like to remember things. Remembering things is often painful. I'd rather do without that pain.

So, is this a true story? Well, I can't guarantee that everything I told you is the truth. I'm sure there's a lie in here somewhere. As far as I know, this is the closest to the truth that I can get.

But, truth is irrelevent, because a story is neither the full truth or a total lie. I guess it's whatever you want it to be–a truth or a lie.

-end
5:04a1oct97

How much there is in books that one does not want to know.
                    -John Burroughs

(**WRITER'S NOTE***: Among Giants is a bit strange. There are parts in it that are true and parts that are straight out lies. I didn't know exactly where it should go in this anthology, because it is neither completely fiction nor non-fiction. It's a bit of both. Now the fun part is figuring out which parts are true and which aren't. Makes you wonder, eh?*)

RANDOM THOUGHTS OF A BLOCKED WRITER

The other day, Jason Brown told me that he wanted me to write a comic book script for him to draw. He said that he could only draw eight pages. I'm not good at doing short stories like that so I told him that if I didn't come up with a story that required eight pages, I would write a full script and he and a group of artist could help work on it. Then I realized, I don't have an idea for a story of any length. So now I'm trying to think of something:

Okay. Allrighty. All right. Here I am. Sitting at the computer, thinking. Once, a female friend of mine asked me if men just have sex on their mind. "What?" I said, as I looked up from staring at her breast. "I didn't hear you. I was thinking about something."
      "Never mind," she said.
      I'm trying to think up a story now. Okay, it's time to get serious. Here it goes. No distractions. Yes in deedy. Fishing for ideas. One will come along any second now. Just waiting. The ideas should be flooding in anytime soon. Waiting... Waiting... Any second now. Waiting... Waiting... Waiting... Waiting... Waiting... Waiting... Fuck! Waiting... Waiting... Waiting... Waiting...
      Waiting............
      I wanted to do a Coyote story but I don't think it's ready yet. He said that he wanted a story full of violence, weird tripped-out shit, and all sorts of fun things like that. So I'm gonna have to make it excessively violent. Blood and guts. EC-styled shit.
      I'm staring at the computer screen, wondering how much radiation is emitting from it and what kind of cancer I'll have in result of it. Big basketball sized tumors coming from my head. I could be the next Elephant Man. Maybe that could be story, a computer that kills people. Okay, go ahead and laugh. I had an idea for this story about a guy (maybe a cop) who saves the life of this transvestite, and he/she feels that he/she is in debt to him. I told one of the artists who was going to assist us my idea, and he looked at me as if I were insane. What do you call a transvestite, anyway? A he or a she. My cousins call them shems.
      Maybe they'll make a movie about it, but it'll be about a generous film star who gives a transvestite a ride home. It'll be titled, *Eddie Murphy, All Around Nice guy.*

Damn, I wish I had some music to listen to. Too bad I don't do drugs. Then I could trip out and maybe some weird idea would come out. Some people say that's when they get their best ideas – when they're stoned out on drugs. I don't know if that's true. The people I see stoned out on drugs usually can't form complete sentences. "Yeah, man. Dig. Wow. Uh..." followed by ten minutes of silence, then, "Cool." And then a lot of laughter.

Wait. I'll be back.

I WENT walking around. I looked at other people on their computers (this is being written in the college computer lab). They probably thought I was crazy. I went to watch a little television. Nothing was on. Some rap video about big booty's and wonderful sex.

I sat beside this one girl and talked to her. She said that all men are all alike. They're all bastards. Then she asked if what all men thought about was sex. I said that I didn't know. She asked if all I think about is sex. I said, "No, sometimes I sleep." Then I dream about sex. Or is that the same thing as thinking about it. I don't think so. Then I wondered what having sex with her would be like.

I sat on the roof, kicked off the moss–then the somebody yelled at me and told me to get off.

I returned to the computer, looked at the map of the United States, wondered how they figure out the borders of each state.

Where's my muse when I need her? She's probably out whoring herself to another writer. The bitch.

Maybe I could do a Frank Miller/Mickey Spillane type story. I don't know.

I would like to do the story about the tabloid writers who interview Satan, but that requires research–reading the bible, shit like that. I'm sick of doing research.

I heard from another writer that if you grab a week's worth of newspapers and read through them completely, somewhere in one of those newspaper articles you can find a story. But I'm too lazy to read one newspaper.

Now my mind is a total blank.

155

Waiting for Godot.

I'm looking at Gabriel, who is sitting beside me on another computer, as he prepares addressing a letter. He asks me what's going on. I say, nothing much. Yes, I do live the exciting life. Don't you wish you were me.

I wonder if people slit their wrist because of things like this. I tell you, I'm about ready to do it. Unfortunately, I have no sharp objects to cut myself with. Maybe I can use paper. Massive paper cut. You can read about it in the news tomorrow. Tvli Jacob dies of a massive paper cut. He nearly severs his own hand off. There'll be pictures and everything. Damn shame. Then people would say, "It was such a surprise that he killed himself. He seemed so happy." They always say that. You don't ever hear them say, "He was such a miserable bastard, I'm not surprised. Hell, I'd've thought he'd do it sooner."

Staring at the wall, staring at the computer. Looking at this computer is deteriorating my eye sight, giving me a bloody headache. Maybe I should do a story about a guy who gets killed by paper cuts. Okay, dumb idea. I've had worse. Actually, the worse ones are the best I get.

Then my mind starts wandering....

Three women and a bottle of whipped cream; my mind returns to thoughts of sex...

FROG DREAMS

To understand the events that occurred when I first went to college, we'll have to travel a couple days back. The date was August 22, 1994. The time was around 10:30 a.m.

I was getting ready to embark on the journey of my life; college! My goodbyes were said to my woman, my folks, and the uncanny "Moe Cat," feline extraordinaire.

Zero hour was upon me. It was time to grow up and take a step closer to manhood. The date was set. The quest was clear, but I had one problem in the form of cargo. We'll just call her Melissa for now.

With '87 Mazda packed to capacity and 2100+ miles of pavement in front of me, I was off. My passenger was the daughter of one of my mom's friends, and for some reason, she thought she was my cousin.

Everything started off cool. The first couple hours were filled with small talk, chit chat, and plain old bullshittin'. It wore damn thin by the time we hit Central Nevada, though, and it was here that it became clear I was facing my first challenge in this "real" world, and the challenge was trying to keep up a conversation with someone who had less personality and communication skills then a newly spaded animal.

"No problem, right Gabe?" I said to myself. I should be able to pull out of this, just sixteen hours to go. Growing up eighteen years in a family like mine seemed to be more than enough conditioning for something like this.

We hit Vegas. Hope was curled up, dead in the back by now. No personality plus no sense of humor added up to a trip through the "sin city" with the devil herself.

Conversing with this chick was like talking to cold strip of bacon that just fell on the floor, slightly amusing but ultimately pointless.

I gave up by the time Flagstaff was in sight. Since coexistence got tossed out the window along with common sense, I started talking to myself with the hopes she'd think I was crazy and maybe she'd jump out.

My discussion topics ranged from missing my girlfriend to what was going on with O.J.. The sight of what I was doing was nothing nice but it kept me kosher 'til we got a room at the

Motel 6 off the freeway in Flagstaff.

In the room I took a shower and laid down on the bed to crash out. That night I had one of the strangest dreams of my life. I was a little fly being chased by a giant frog with Garfield-like eyes. I flapped my little wings as hard as I could but couldn't fly fast enough. Its sticky tongue stuck to the back of me and reeled me in for the kill. It held me up, looked me up and down with a huge eyeball and then, just before it ate me, it said, "Wait a minute...aren't you my cousin?"

I woke up in a hurry and jumped in my truck leaving the deeper meanings of the dream sunk in the cheap sheets I had slept on. No small talk, no fake smiles, or this pretend "cousin" bullshit, this was a mission mission. Get to college was all I was knew.

Hitting the gas, hitting the road, and only hitting the passenger when necessary was the conduct code for the final 9 hours of driving. Aside from the dream, slumber did me good and toned down my militancy. You might even say I was in a "giving mood." It was this passive mood that allowed me to grant the cargo's request for a smoke. A reasonable request, except for the fact that she decided to disregard the ashtray in the truck and use the window instead.

By some spiteful act of god, the ashes flew back in and burnt the hell out of my head. The combination between the burning pain and the smell of burnt hair lynched what was left of a conscience and turned my attention to just the road.

There was no talking. Just thinking and driving, at times vice versa, I kept cool only stopping for gas and occasional relief on the side of the road.

When we finally made it through Gallup, NM, I was a machine. I lived to drive and drove to live.

Albuquerque came and went with the change of a CD. I could care less about UNM, TD's, or any other opportunity I'd have to score with Latinas, my favorite addiction.

After such a long time without interaction, I felt I should say something so I told her to roll up her window. For some reason, executing brute authority in a situation like that made me feel a lot better.

Hope was reborn upon seeing a sign that said, "Santa

Fe 20." It looked like I was gonna make it. I caught myself
before cracking a smile, I figured I didn't need to press my luck.
Maybe when Santa Fe was actually in sight. I punched the gas
in a last ditch effort to make her think I went loco. I didn't
care about life, but nothing was gonna stop me from making it.

SANTA FE!!! At last I passed the test and exorcised
the demons. The frog, the wannabee-cousin bitch I wanted to
just leave on the side of the road would now be out of my face.

It all ended pretty civil. We pulled in to the Motel 6 off
Cerrillos. After we paid for the room, the episode was over.
She went and stayed with some friends she had in town and I
just crashed. I thanked her for giving me directions to the
school and pitching in for gas.

In closing, I'd like to give special thanks to all 7-11
stores along I-91, brothel workers for the massage that kept me
out of prison, and most of all my now deceased Mazda B-
2000(aka THE SILVER BULLET), may god rest his tired soul.

THE ROAD TO PARADISE

My heart sank as I looked at the mountains around me. They were quickly engulfed in the white that threatened to ruin the spring semester of my junior year. Of course, I could've caught another flight as soon as the storm let up, but that wasn't the point. Teachers on the committee had fought to get me to go on this trip; nothing was going to ruin it for me. We could barely see the highway as we drove into Albuquerque. This was going to be the most important day of my life, the scariest too. I would be leaving my mom all alone for five whole months.

The horrible white stuff kept right on falling as we walked into the airport. We met up with the other two kids and their families after I had checked in and got my ticket. We all sat around and looked out the windows or shyly at each other. I didn't really know either one of the other students, so it was pretty awkward. But we would soon realize that we all had our stories. As the time for us to leave got closer, the boy's mom started to cry. I'd heard rumors about her being loose, but I don't know if they were true. His nineteen-year old sister, and two kids, also started crying.

I knew that me and Marlee were going to hit it off. We were both only there with our mothers; no whole family to come and support us. Her mother also began to cry; she was going to be spending the five months helping a boy go through his initiation in the kiva. Me and my mom sat and laughed. She got a little misty-eyed when it was time for me to get on the plane, but we wouldn't cry. We'd both learned somehow that tears didn't help anything. We did the whole "I love you," "Do good in school" thing, I kissed her on the cheek and disappeared down the corridor.

Marlee and I settled in our seats and prepared ourselves for the short taxi to Phoenix. We talked a little bit about whether we were afraid or not, and how much we were gonna miss our mutual friends. We looked at the magazines and every other pamphlet in the seat pocket. Then, after we were about to land in Phoenix, we wondered where Cory was sitting.

We only had twenty minutes before our plane for San Diego left. As soon as we stepped off the plane we were going the wrong way. We wandered around for twenty minutes, me and Marlee talking the whole time, Cory wandering in his own little world. We finally made Cory assume his role as "the man" and had him ask somebody where we were supposed to be. He refused weakly until we ganged up on him. He came back from asking a security guy and whispered that we were to ride the shuttle bus to terminal three; way over somewhere. We stepped outside into the humid air to wait for the shuttle; all of us decked out in pants, long sleeve shirts, sweatshirts, and big coats. It was about ninety degrees there. The driver pushed the pedal down as far as he could without getting cited, and we ran into the terminal. Marlee immediately asked someone to point us in the right direction. We ran, Marlee helping me with my three huge carry-ons. We watched Cory get swallowed into the crowd at the back of the plane, then settled into our seats again. We continued our conversation about how much we were going to miss our friends and how we couldn't wait to get there. As we arrived in San Diego, there were more pools; big houses with pools in every back yard. "Must be nice," Marlee said.

We had an hour to waste in San Diego. Me and Marlee decided to get something to eat, I don't even know what Cory did. We went to this little Pizza Hut Express place and continued to work on our bond. This time the topic of conversation was Cory. I was trying really hard to be nice to him, but he wasn't responsive. "He's got a huge crush on you. That's all there is to it," Marlee laughed. I threw a piece of napkin in her soda. We decided to go wait where we were to board. Cory was nowhere around. So, we sat, surrounded by our five bags, and studied the people we were about to get on this last plane with.

Chinese, Japanese, and Filipinos. They were the majority of the passengers. Of course there were the usual tourists, anxious to get a glimpse of the paradise. Every now and then Marlee would turn and whisper some "Chinese" to me. We'd laugh really quick and then get serious before anybody felt that we were laughing at them. Cory finally showed up, but all the seats were taken so he sat by himself across the room.

We weren't really intentionally mean to him. We had tried to be nice, but he was just too serious. He had tried to take charge when we landed in San Diego, telling us how much time we had to eat, but we just laughed at him. It was just difficult to take him seriously after the way he had wimped out in Phoenix. His story was pretty complicated. We knew that his father had left the family when Cory was pretty young, but we wouldn't find out the depth of it until we had been gone for a couple months.

We weren't happy when it was time to board. This flight was going to be for five whole hours. We piled on among all the tourists and Chinese people. Luckily, the lady that was in charge of setting everything up for us had put me and Marlee together on everything, all our flights, our sponsors, and our dorms. For the final time, we sat down together and started talking. The plane was one of the huge ones you see the "Growing Pains" family traveling on. We laughed the whole time we were filling out our agriculture cards; as if a couple of seventeen-year olds would be smuggling in fruit. We didn't even know the address of the place we were going. We bought head phones and watched Forrest Gump, ate our dinner, then sat for the next two hours staring off into space. Looking out the window had gotten dissappointing after the first twenty minutes. It was five hours of waves beneath us. We'd seen enough. With nothing left to do, we decided to write letters to a couple of our friends. A steward passed by and panicked because we were writing on the barf bags. He politely asked us not to, and brought us some stationary with the airline company's name on it.

Finally, we landed. It was amazing to see the island come up out of nowhere. It looked pretty normal from the sky, besides the fact that it was so green. Me and Marlee sat and waited while all the Japanese, Filipinos, and tourists scrambled off the plane. We jumped up as soon as there was room for us to stand in the aisle. One of my enormous bags was stuck behind a bunch of other people's, so Marlee gave me a quick hug and headed off the plane. I caught up to her in the corridor and we walked side-by-side. We must have looked at each other about twenty times.

When we stepped off the plane, there were twelve students and a couple of adults waiting for us. They were all holding signs with our names and leis to give to us. We were rushed by them when they realized it was us; Cory was standing behind all of them with his three leis. The kisses on the cheek when we recieved our leis were special because it wasn't a tourist thing coming from these people. It was sincere because it was their tradition. They took our bags and surrounded us as we walked from the terminal to the baggage claim. Once again we were enveloped by the humid air, but this was far worse. I could feel it on my skin. We had to explain that we almost didn't make it because of the huge storm.

While we were waiting for our bags to come onto one of the six carousels, I discovered that the reason I had received so many leis and signs was because all of the girls were from my dorm. The plans for me and Marlee to be in the same dorm had fallen through, which was okay. We were both pretty friendly and could manage ourselves, as long as we saw each other once in a while. Cory, on the other hand, was barely talking to the guys from his dorm. They had to squeeze information out of him.

When we were in front of the main entrance to the airport they showed us the place that was to be our home for the next five months. There it was, way on the top of this mountain. It reminded me of a queen up there, all in white amongst the green trees. It was unbarably hot by now, so we made our way to the cars. Me, Marlee, and all the girls piled into a station wagon with our Dorm Assistant and Mr. Ako, our main sponsor. We got onto the highway and made our way up the mountain, to the school. They pointed out different sites, but I have no idea what they were now. My head was swimming with all the events of the day.

I couldn't see what the place was like when we got there because it was so dark. I was dropped off because my dorm was about in the middle of the mountain; Marlee would be way at the top. So, the girls jumped out and grabbed my stuff. I said goodbye to Mr. Ako and quietly followed them down the steps to the dorm. They led me up the five steps to the second floor, showed me the office and my little pocket on the door where I was to sign out. There was a little greeting party in there and a whirlwind of giggles and hugs surrounded me. Then, we made our way up the steps across from the office to the third floor. My room was near the end of the hall and excited heads popped out of doors along the way, "Is she here yet?" "Is that her?" I smiled shyly at the voices, and continued down the hall. One of the girls opened the door to my room, and I stepped in. There was a bouquet of roses in a basket on the desk. There was a small balloon with a happy face on it. When I turned around to thank somebody, my bags were lined up neatly along the wall, and the door was closed. I walked over to the flowers and looked at the card:

Welcome Tianausdi

Love the girls of Kapuaiwa

I gently took my leis off and hung them on the door knob of my closet. That was all I needed. I could make this place home. These girls were no different from my friends at home. I just didn't know them yet. I looked around my little closet room. There was barely enough space for me to walk around. My twin bed was pushed all the way to the window, the back wall, right against the right wall. A milk carton, with a small blue lamp on it, was my bedside table. The closet was in the left corner, by the window. The counter/desk was in the space between where my closet stuck out, and my neighbor's closet stuck out. It wasn't a whole lot of room, but it was all mine. No rowdy roommates to keep me up until three in the morning.

"Um, hi. I was wondering if you wanted to come over and visit." A smiling face was at my screen. I was greatful for the offer and followed her into the next room. I don't know who was all in there. It took me a couple of days to get used to some of the Hawaiian names, so I don't really remember anybody from the first night. They were sitting around talking, and a few of them were eating food in take-out boxes from the cafeteria. I was offered some, but I didn't know what it was yet, so I refused. I did accept the drink I was offered. Guava juice was to be my first love in Hawai'i. I loved the way the sweetness teased my tongue before it slid down my throat. I sat there, in my own little world, falling in love with the guava juice. A head popped in the door and announced it was time for the meeting. I was to be presented officially. I followed the girls down the back stairs to the first floor. We passed through the laundry room and went by the kitchen.

The lounge was an open space with a concrete floor painted red. There were two little areas wet up with couches, chairs, and televisions on blue carpets just big enough to hold the furniture. All heads turned when I walked in, my head went down. The D.A.'s stood up and gave me welcome speeches; there were three of them. Then, it was my turn to introduce myself to the Kapuaiwa dorm. I stood up and told a little about myself: the reading, the soccer, the cross country, the music, whatever. Then, we had to play a game about commercial jingles. I don't remember what it was about. It was kind of dumb. After that torture was over, I sat at a table with Melanie's friends. I've never wished for anybody as much as I wished for Melanie that night. She was one of the Hawaiian girls that had gone over to my school for the fall semester. We became fast friends when she saw me crying after my mom left me at the Indian school the first night. We had done everything together; she talked me into playing soccer. Now here I was all alone, sitting with her friends, talking about what it was like where I was from. It was study hall time, so we were sent to our rooms for the rest of the night. My new group of friends had decided they would wait for me to go to breakfast the next day.

So, here I was, on this island in the middle of the ocean. I couldn't believe it. And the study hall thing blew my mind; seven thirty to eleven o'clock every school night. Plus, having to get up at about five in the morning, shower, and do my detail, dumping the trash, before going to breakfast at seven; mandatory also. But I would be okay. My new friends would help me out. I wondered how Marlee had made out. I was sure she did fine. Now, it was midnight at home and I was tired. I had a long day of new student stuff ahead of me. So I passed out in my clothes, and didn't wake up until I heard a voice at the screen of my door.

HAIRSTYLIST

One deep breath as I pulled my bag over my shoulder. Another day another dollar. I wondered how life would be if I wasn't a Hairstylist. What could I be if I were to pick a new life or career? To tell you the truth, my career is my life. Maybe that's why it isn't so hard to go to work every day. Walking to my car, passing people smile at me. I think I remember you. I think. I reach into my pocket at the stop lights, thank goodness for tips. I don't like to cook anymore, no more domesticated woman. Can you believe it, the money I'm making , working part-time? The tips! No social service case number! No man to run my life! Maybe I reached my goal in life.

How did I come to be this Hairstylist? I think when I went to Fort Sill Indian School in Oklahoma. I was about 14 years old. The school had two dormitories, one for boys and one for girls. My grandma lived in the town of Lawton, Oklahoma. I had so much fun at school. I hardly saw my grandma. The fall weather was still hot and muggy; it was easy to ignore and get used to it when you're young. Every hour or so we could hear the thunderous booms from Fort Sill Army Base. What I remember the most was the rain storms and tornado watches. In those days our matrons kept us inside and ready to run to the cafeteria basement. My friends and I would stay in our rooms putting on makeup, curling our hair and talking about guys. We always ignored the perfectly handsome guys at our school and went for the guys at Riverside Indian School. Causing chaos was always fun. Once, I saw an Indian girl at the Fort Sill vs Riverside football game with yellowish feathered back hair and I just had to have my hair like that. My hair, was long and straight. It was ugly, just black as can be. My dad always said it was bad luck to cut your hair, "You might make someone in our family sick if you cut it!" he'd say. My dad was this tall, muscular Arapaho man, with a huge voice. I wasn't scared of him tho', and he knew it. He would shake his head at me and say, "Aline take care of your daughter, she don't listen to me!" But we were best friends.

So like I was saying, me and my homegirl Annie went and stole a frosting kit at the mall. We read all the directions And put it all over my hair. We followed the directions but my hair turned reddish orange. In our rooms we had only lights by the closet and the drawers, so it was really hard to tell how red I was. I went to bed since our matrons kept hollering at us. All my buddies lied to me when they said I looked okay, so I went to breakfast thinking so. With my friends I felt comfortable and soon forgot my hair. Then a group of guys came, the loud guys! One guy, a short stalky football player, could of been handsome if he wasn't a pest, glanced at me. That was it, they RAZZED me so bad. They said I was copying the black women down in Nigger Town, They said my hair looked like a dog. I didn't know what to do, I had to pretend it was cool. In the future, I decided, I'm going to do it on someone else.

Like my other "Homey", Iris. She always wanted to be different, she was different. On all our rez, no one had freckles all over their face. Me and my sisters had to whoop ass when other girls made fun of her. Her face was white and her hair was wavy. We liked Chaka Khan so bad, the way she dressed, her platform shoes and her music. Then this one Indian girl from the City came after her little sister, she was dressed exactly like Chaka Khan. She had a long leather jacket, platform shoes, had the biggest flairs on her pants and an afro. We looked at each other in unison and shook our head. Uh uh, we couldn't be beat. I decided I was going to do a "Fro" on Iris, she didn't say one way or the other if she wanted it. I only had to cut off about 8 inches of hair, then we permed the hell out of it. We used the smallest rods we could find. I wasn't all to blame at the time, since she called her Grandfather and he sent her money for supplies. Her so called "Fro" looked more like a Brillo pad, but I couldn't tell her. The football mob did the same thing to her that they did to me. However, she wasn't a strong person as I. She cried and cried until I told her I would do her a frost. This time she was a big hit. Until we went home, some girls would go home for the weekends and come back with a blonde afro.

I always had this picture in my mind of the Indians coming to town, the women in their shawls, a part straight down their head, greased up braids, right behind their men. Then the white people saying, "Put the good things away, the Indians are coming to town, watch for the stealers!" then there was always this good do'er white lady that thought she was a good Samaritan, talking loud as hell like Indians couldn't hear. So I always wanted to change the typical look. I used to tell my little sister, "You can't hang around us, because you look fresh off the rez!" and "The only part you should have, is down your crack!" Her and her friends would have a shit fit. I decided I would let my little sister hang out with us, but we had to do something about her dorky look. I let Iris tweeze her Russian looking eyebrows and we frosted her hair blondish, by this time we were real good. The bad thing about this was, she turned out real pretty. She took all the attention, we used to get. We could never get rid of her after that.

My parents would be waiting for us at the bus depot, my mom would be filled with excitement, and dad, he wasn't sure what to expect. It was a good feeling to know my mom accepted me for who I was. My dad was too traditional. He probably wanted me to marry the chief's son. We didn't have Chiefs anymore, so I wouldn't even consider the Chief of Police's son.

My mom would get her hair done weekly at the beauty shop. When we were at the pow wows, it would be a problem for her. For me, it was no problem at all. Sometimes we would be gone for weeks, she soon learned to trust me. When word got out, all her friends would be lining up at our camp. They did their best to look their best, but the pow wow dust managed to coat them with a dusty brown cast. I know I was responsible for all the Indian ladies blocking the way for others to watch at the pow wow because of this nice lookin' bubble of a hairstyle in their way. My father would soon learn to tolerate me and my changing ways.

One year coming home from the school, I was amazed and shocked to see my father. "You look like Will Sampson! Your hair is long!" he had it in a short pony tail. I was amazed to see this rigid ol'skin with long hair. Me and my sisters kept braiding our dad's hair and calling him a "Hippy", til he seen my tattoos.

"Those better come off, you hear!", he hollered. "Our family doesn't have tattoos!" Damn you and your damn traditions, I dared not say. My parents argued and waved hands. "Talk to your daughters."

Sadly, I felt I caused the fatal accidents that took my parent's life. Earliest hours of the morning , screeching, scraping, bending and the most piercing sent telepathic waves to me as I sat up in my dorm room while at University of Wyoming. It was over in a split second, so I thought nothing of it. Later in the breakfast line, the looked on Kendall's face, and it told me what I felt. The funeral days were a blur, I didn't know who came or went. My skin on my face felt thick; my eyelids did not want to open clearly and I walked like I was being pushed around. "Debino!" I heard all the old ladies chanting those eerie death songs. I heard chanting, then one of my grandpas pull at my hair, cutting it off. It was part of the mourning ritual, that's what woke me out of my daze.

I had some bad years after; it never occurred to me to blame my haircutting. Every time I seen a friend, I knew exactly what I should do with their hair. At one time I found myself single, with three children and no job. I panicked, but I felt comfort knowing I could do hair. I went to look for a job, not realizing you needed a Cosmetology license. With my little family we found ourselves living in Colorado. It was actually an attempt for me and my ex husband to reconcile in another town. We didn't know that it would be a new direction for me.

DRAMA

CINDERELLA'S GLASS SLIPPER

Ginger

> _sits sideways on a wooden chair in
> the middle of the stage, erect posture,
> leaning forward slightly_

See my shoes. These are the shoes I wore from the hospital ...

> _pointing toes, lifting leg lightly_

I carried Lily home in these shoes... She was wrapped tight in
a blanket ... It was kinda' cloudy that day, but I held her real
close to my chest ... She was a beautiful baby. A good baby...
Never cried a lot. Slept all night. An angel from heaven ... You
should see her now. Beautiful child. Real bright in school. She
comes home and says, "Mommy, mommy look what I made."
... I tell ya. That child swells me full of pride ... (Pause.) Yup,
the soles of these shoes carry me back to my wedding day.

> _looking down at shoes_

This was before Lily of course. But I'll never forget that day...
Frank is the one who picked these for me. When we were in the
shoe store, he was down on his knees in front of me and when
he took the shoe box from the sales lady; you should have seen
the light in his eyes. I halfway thought he bought them for
himself.

> _bends leg back and slips the shoe off.
> runs finger along the edge;
> carefully examines it_

Now they're not so new anymore.

> _bends leg back and slips shoe
> back on; looks down at it, lifting leg
> slightly_

173

But right there in that store ... I remember his exact words ... "Ginger," he said, "You know we've been together for five years. I know that with me being Indian you went through a lot ... but I know if we stick together the way we have been, it doesn't matter what my nationality ... you are my life. I love you and always want to be with you ... Will you marry me?" ... Ooh, he gave me everything, more than I ever expect. He is the only man for me ... (Pause.) Then we moved to California and did it!

> *showing wedding band to audience*

And thank God. I have of died if I had never met him.

> *looks toward ceiling*

I had been living on the streets for years. Just hanging with the girls on Tango Boulevard. I guess the white skin tight dress really caught his eye. That's his favorite ...

> *looks toward audience*

and it goes well with these shoes and that little silk black vest I have ... (Pause)

> *crosses legs*

I used to be called "Bambi" ... but Frank said I was delicious and he started calling me, "Ginger." It stuck and was official weeks before the wedding. He said that was the name of his late aunt who raised him in the south projects since birth ... I was real attracted to his supple brown skin (Pause.) Yup, these shoes sure do bring back a lot of memories.

> *gets up, slips shoes off, pulls off t h e fake eyelashes, walks from the chair, back turned to the audience, unzips the back of the dress, slips dress off, removes wig, drops to floor, unfastens b r a and drops to floor, walks of wearing only a jock. Lights out.*

INDIAN BALL

*A tall Indian girl limps as
she walks back and forth
with a basketball, waiting
for the bus to arrive. It is
late at night probably the
last bus leaving that
night.*

They made me do this! It was all supposed to be fun; we talked about sportmanship, walking tall and proud. Now I feel I should disappear! It's everywhere--how basketball was put on top, I don't know. Honor or disgrace has the worst, or should I say the most powerful of unwritten rules. I was born into a family of basketball players. I guess as Indians, we could no longer prove ourselves proud as our ancestors did. The only challenge we had to prove to the Creator as worthy and proud, was to become the best in a game of basketball. When my dad was my age they probably traveled on horse and wagon. It was St. Stephens against St. Michaels. They couldn't count coup so they counted 1st place trophies. Even the Newas shouted on the sides as they do now. -20 weather and driving on icy roads, they're still there. An' they seen me, The whole tribe probably. I missed a shot. My sis Bubba, she'd hate me. Yes, she was full of All Tourney trophies, like the rest of my family. *You and me sis, we have something in common, we're gone!* Out of 7 daughters, maybe 5 played on dad's team. It isn't my GAME, I tell them. I miss shots for a purpose, I act stupid for a reason. He doesn't get it, dad says we have to prove our team the best! I think, he had to prove HIS team is the best. Arapaho's are tall because we are Arapaho. The Creator did not make us tall for basketball. One stupid game and it's me who should leave.

*She sets the ball on the
bench and boards the bus*

FAMILY TIES

Actors:

Don
Jay
Sheila

> *Outside a large two story
> house. At a large family
> gathering. 10 to 15 cars
> are parked outside
> making it impossible to
> leave.*

Dave: I had to get out of there! It's really bad that they need to do that. When they start to gossip, we need a can of bullshit

> *They share a cigarette, as
> they sit on the hood of a
> 74' Mercury Cougar.*

Jay: Yeah, we spiked the punch with the "Smart Ass Cure" too. You heard Sheila E (easy) dogging Odee about being pregnant at 15. Someone forgets how they earned her name!

> *Two small boys take a
> cigarette from the pack.
> A different girl watches
> and takes two from the
> pack also*

Dave: I dare you to go up there and ask her how many of those husbands she's had (eyebrows raised).

Jay: For a case and fifth?

> *They both laugh and
> notice the half empty
> pack of Marlboros.*

Dave: You already owe me that, so we're even. Plus the

cigarettes you're stealing.

> *Two little boys run by*
> *and try to steal sips of*
> *the guys' beer.*

DAVE: Look at those two! Who's blind not to notice they're brothers? They both have the ears and nose like ScrewGene (Eugene).

> *The boys slurp their*
> *noses and wipe it on*
> *their cheeks at the same*
> *time.*

Jay: They even act like him! My sister is fuckin' stupid. If she likes being fucked, it's her problem. As long as ScrewGene keeps the green in my pocket.

> *Sheila sneaks up on the*
> *little boys, 'til she hears*
> *the conversation of the*
> *two guys. She knocks*
> *their beer off the hood*

Sheila: He looks like his dad! Ya'll bitch worse than women (staring madly). When he comes back from the army, he's going to kick ya'lls ass. Don't mess with my son! an' why'd you give him beer?

Jay: Shut your hole! If that was his dad, he'd be nappy. I think that army man is going to kick your ass!

> *She puts her hands into*
> *her pockets and squeezes*
> *in between the two guys.*
> *An' later offers them a*
> *cigarette a piece.*

Sheila: Ya'll keep your mouth shut for me? P...L...E...A...S...E...? It's hard enough for me (looks sad). Okay? (pause) Ya'll want to party tonight? We'll party tonight. Okay? My soldier sent me some big cash.

PEPTO

(A young Chicano male stands
center stage in a fast food
uniform with grease on the front.
He's holding, sitting down on a
couch.)

Yeah, well, $4.25 an hour didn't say much about the
job at first, but it kept my Old lady off my back, you know? It
was work, so what could she say?

When I first went in, they started me off at the
dunking-fries-machine, so I made 'papas' for the first month I
was there. I'd come home late all the time and the Old lady'd
bitch me out for trying to climb stinking like burnt papas. _A la
verga_! Sometimes, you just can't win, bro, you know?.

After about a month more of that, Freddy the Manager
moved me onto making ensaladas. I hated that shit, bro'.
Cutting those pinche' tomatoes, the mamon cabbage, and that
shitty lettuce. Then the people at work would start their shit
too, "This salad's not crispy enough," "There's too much
Caesar on this." Damn bro', I tried to tell them it wasn't my
fault. It wasn't like I was one of those Mojados out in the field
picking the shit, you know? Late at night I'd come home and
try to snuggle up to my Old Lady and she said I was too cold.
"No shit," I told her, "I'm trying to warm up, A LA VERGA!"

The next month, I started training on the burgers. I
picked it up real easy. All you had to do was throw the meat
on the grill then put it in the bun. A third grader could do that
shit, bro'.

On one of the slow nights I got off early then came
home. I went inside the house and took off my shoes so I
could watch some wrestling on T.V.. The old Lady was in the
back room and I didn't wanna wake her, so I kept the T.V.
Real low, you know.

I felt all greasy, so I went to wash up. I heard the Old
Lady wimpering around like she was crying, so I went to see
what was the matter. I walked up to the door then peeked
inside.

179

Now, you know I seen some fucked up shit in my life bro'. Where I grew up wasn't no paradise, you know, but goddamn, bro', I damn near shit my pants when I seen my neighbor's 'gorda' wife 'mowing *mi esposa's* lawn like the last supper. She had her legs up like Bugs Bunny. "A LA VERGA!" I said to myself, " What the fuck do I do?" Do I get pissed and go whip that *puta's* ass or just kick back and watch? If I do go in there, which *puta's* ass do I kick?

I think I could'a handled it better if I saw Sancho in there, bro'. At least then I would know to go in there and kick the shit out of him, but this? What was I supposed to do with a chick, bro?!

Rather than break it up, I just did the only thing I could do: watch. *Claro*, I wasn't gonna watch that Gorda and my Old Lady bump *chingaderas* and kiss around on an empty stomach, so I fixed a sandwich and grabbed a cerveza outta the fridge.

I'll give that *pinche'* Gorda some credit though, bro'. She got some wind. A la, she was down there so long that I wondered if she was still breathing. I went back outside to make it loud like I just pulled up. Then I gave the Gorda five minutes to sneak out the back while I walked up in the front.

I walked in and laid next to the Old Lady like always. As usual, no *sexo*. I got up to go take *mierdo*. I was feeling kinda sick so I opened up the medicine cabinet. I didn't know what happened, so I asked my wife, "Hey, what happened to the Pepto?"

Dolphin

De Armond Williams